Betty said to:
Please enjoy redding
And pass on—si...
when finished

Betty Turner (John)

I Will Lift Up My Eyes

The Power of Praise and Prayer

May God bless you indeed.

by

Ann Davis Melton

Ann D. Melton

WestBow
PRESS
A DIVISION OF THOMAS NELSON

Prov. 3:6

WestBow Press books may be ordered through booksellers or by contacting:

WestBow Press
A Division of Thomas Nelson
1663 Liberty Drive
Bloomington, IN 47403
www.westbowpress.com
1-(866) 928-1240

ISBN: 978-1-4497-8870-4 (sc)
ISBN: 978-1-4497-8871-1 (hc)
ISBN: 978-1-4497-8869-8 (e)

Library of Congress Control Number: 2013904831

Printed in the United States of America.

WestBow Press rev. date: 04/04/2013

Acknowledgments

This book is the result of the friendship, encouragement, and support of many people. First, I want to thank my husband, Frank; my children, Myra and Buddy; and my first cousin, Mary Katherine Lowder (who is really more like a sister than a cousin) for their willingness to share with so many others the story of God's gracious dealings with our family. Living in a glass house is not easy. Next, I offer my deepest appreciation to all my wonderful friends who have been willing to share their joys, sorrows, heartaches, and victories in this book: Tina and John Stovall, Linda Minor, Kathy Whiteside, Ann Ledford, Ann Culpepper, and Lorraine Lee. I want to thank several of these same folks for their patience as they also helped me critique my work.

I want to especially thank two very special ladies. First, Doris Howard for the many hours she spent reading and rereading the text checking for errors when she had so many more important things to do, like filling shoe boxes for Operation Christmas Child. And second, I want to thank Susan Kingshill for giving her time to this project when she had so many critical family issues to deal with during the busy holiday season. Their love of the Lord and their patience with me has put them both right up there with Job in my eyes. My thanks also to my sister Vikki Ganger for all her wonderful ideas! She is really the writer in the family!

And a special thanks to Dr. John Bunn, pastor emeritus at Sylva First Baptist, for his encouragement. I don't believe I would ever have published this book if he had not believed in its value or worth.

Table of Contents

"I waited patiently for God to help me; then he listened and heard my cry. He … set my feet on a hard, firm path and steadied me as I walked along. He has given me a new song to sing, of praises to our God. Now many will hear of the glorious things he did for me, and stand in awe before the Lord, and put their trust in him."

Psalm 40:1-3 LB

Preface

*I*n the following pages I have shared with you some very personal times in my life and in the lives of family and friends. It is my hope that they will provide a small measure of help in your journey - that because of these stories you will be encouraged to pursue a close personal relationship with the Lord. I have shared some stories that I and others would rather have forgotten, but I believe that it is in our mistakes, heartaches, sorrows, and victories that we learn some of our most valuable lessons. I have recorded all these stories in an effort to glorify God.

I hope that through these stories you will come to see that prayer and praise can change your life. The time you spend with the Lord in prayer can re-energize you and renew your spirit. It can renew your mind and body and provide healing. Prayer can calm the greatest storms in your life and leave you better able to cope with the stresses of day-to-day living.

Prayer and praise bring you into the presence of God. After only a few moments of sitting quietly, talking with him and listening for his direction, you will find comfort and peace. As time goes by and you continue to meet the Lord in prayer each day, you will discover that your eyes are gradually opened to his word and that you will begin to grow in wisdom and understanding. However, prayer does not need proof. It needs practice.

It is also my hope that the reader will see that the Bible is not some antiquated document but a holy book filled with the timely words of God. It has the power to meet your every need and to help you in your gravest hours. It has wonderful examples of prayers. It is filled with promises – powerful promises. To open the Bible is like opening a treasure chest filled with promises, hope, and wisdom that can change your life in wonderful ways. It is my prayer that the scripture passages given in this book will serve to whet your appetite and cause you to search the scriptures yourself for those verses that fit your needs.

I pray that after you read this book you will be filled with a longing for a closer relationship with God. My promise to the reader is that if you will take the time to develop a close personal relationship with the Lord, your life will never be the same again. Instead, your life will be filled with miracles – daily miracles. Your life will be more exciting than that of any action hero you have ever seen on the silver screen. I promise you that the lives of characters like Indiana Jones will in no way compare to the excitement of your life. Each morning when you open your eyes and begin your day, you will do so in great anticipation, waiting to see what God has in store for you – what miracles he will perform. In your adventure you will find increased hope, renewed spirit, new friends, a stronger faith, deeper commitment, greater love, and peace – a peace that will pass all understanding.

A song that I love says, "It is no secret what God can do, what he's done for others he can do for you." I encourage you to step out in faith, claim his promises, and go to him in prayer asking for what you need. Praise him, spend time with him, give him the glory and honor that he deserves, and watch the miracles come into your life. I pray that you will come to see how wide, how long, how high, and how deep God's love really is and will experience his love for yourself.

"It is my pleasure to tell you about the miraculous signs and wonders that the Most High God has performed for me. How great are his signs, how mighty his wonders! His kingdom is an eternal kingdom; his dominion endures from generation to generation."

Daniel 4:2-3 NIV

Praise Him

A person's life can change forever in the blink of an eye. Such was the case when my cell phone rang and I answered it only to hear the panic and fear in the voice of Carla, our daughter-in-law. "Buddy's been in an accident! He had just loaded some cattle onto a truck and was shutting the heavy steel gate when a cow kicked the gate, causing it to crash into his face."

"Where is he now?" I asked.

"He has been transported to the trauma unit in Asheville."

"We'll pack our things and be on the road in an hour," I assured her. Nine hours later we walked into our son's hospital room. Once there it didn't take us long to realize that we were listening to a miracle unfold.

"I knew the injury was really serious," Buddy said, "and I was afraid that I was going to black out. No one knew where I was or what I was doing. If I had blacked out, I could have bled to death before anyone found me, and the cattle could have come off the truck and trampled me."

But the Lord was with him in that pasture because he was able to lock the gate to keep the cattle on the truck and then call

911 on his cell phone. This was amazing as there are few places on that mountain where one can get cell phone reception.

After calling for help, Buddy knew that he had to somehow get from the barn and down the mountain to his house so that if he blacked out he would do so in his yard where help would find him. Miraculously, he was able to do just that.

Surgery was scheduled and would involve three teams of surgeons: neurosurgeons who would do two craniotomies to remove the bone fragments that had cut into the lining of the brain allowing the spinal fluid to leak, maxi-facial surgeons who would work to reconstruct the damage to his face, and plastic surgeons who would work to rebuild the nose and the bone between the eyes.

My son was taken down to surgery at 6:30 Sunday morning. When the surgery began, it soon became apparent that Buddy's injuries were far worse than the CT scans had indicated. An ordeal that was expected to last five and a half hours lasted eleven.

The surgery went well. After one day in ICU, he was moved to a step-down unit with hopes that he would be able to go home on Thursday. However, by Thursday Buddy's condition had worsened. He was on three different painkillers: morphine, oxycodone, and Percocet. Even these failed to relieve the pain. Still, we remained hopeful and prayed that he would be able to go home on Sunday. But by then he was much worse. The pain was now accompanied by nausea and vomiting even though he had not eaten in nine days, and he was running a fever. His white blood count was high, and the doctors could not determine the location of the infection. That Sunday will live forever as one of the worst days of my life.

When the accident first happened, I had called a minister friend, Ron Childress, who has the gift of healing. At 11:30 that

Sunday night, he called me. "I have called to pray for your son... I'm going to ask God to send a healing angel to him."

At 9:00 the next morning when I walked into my son's room, Carla looked up from his bedside. "How was your night?" I whispered. She replied, "We had a really good night; Buddy slept all night and so did I." I was relieved to hear this but was totally unprepared for what she said next.

Carla went on, "I have to tell you, Jesus visited us last night!"

"It was around 11:30. Buddy was asleep. The room was dark, and I had my eyes closed. I was praying so hard. I was so afraid, so worried, so sad and heart-broken for Buddy when suddenly I realized that a light had come on in the room.

Carla continued, "I opened my eyes and Jesus was standing on the other side of Buddy's bed. His face was so bright that I couldn't see his features, but I know he was smiling at me. He laid both hands on Buddy's chest. In a few moments, he was gone! "

I stood there hardly moving. I was in awe! I remember thinking about the passage in Luke 2:19 KJV that says, "But Mary kept all these things, and pondered them in her heart." All day I pondered Carla's experience in *my* heart. All day I contemplated the presence of Jesus at my son's bedside, and I thanked him again and again for such grace, mercy, and love.

That day we had Buddy up most of the day. Our goal was to get him to eat. All day we would push him to eat tiny bits of Jell-O or take small sips of a protein drink. When his supper tray came, he thought he could eat something. I had just given him one bite when suddenly he lost everything he had eaten that day. As soon as I could, I called my minister friend again to ask him to continue to pray for my son.

"Listen to me!" my friend said emphatically. "You must be

praising God for the healing that is taking place in your son's body right now!" Seven times he repeated this, each time with greater emphasis than the time before. After getting off the phone, I went back into my son's room and told Carla what he had said.

Buddy is a member of Balsam Range, an internationally known bluegrass band. Thousands of people were following his progress and were praying for him. When I reported what the minister had told me, Carla immediately got on the internet and asked everyone to join us in praising God for the healing that was already taking place in Buddy's body.

After the accident happened, I had thanked God that Buddy had not been killed. I had thanked God that he had not blacked out and had been able to call for help. I thanked him for many things at that time. And, of course, after the surgery, I thanked him that it had gone so well. I thanked God for the wonderful doctors. But I must confess that as the days went by, when the pain was so terrible, when Buddy continued to get worse, and when he got an infection, I spent my time praying for the pain to go away and for his fever to break. I was so busy asking God for things that I spent little time thanking him, and I know that I did not praise him.

At 5:30 the next morning, I received a text message from Carla which read: "Amazing! This is the most amazing thing! Buddy jumped out of bed and is walking around the room, whistling, and cracking jokes. He had no pain medication all night." He remained pain free most of that day and was able to eat breakfast and lunch. The next day he was pain free all day and ate anything he wanted. The following day he went home and that evening was in the recording studio with the other members of Balsam Range.

"Amazing" since we had been told that his recovery would take a minimum of six months! "Amazing" that once I stopped asking God for things, and began praising him, my son's condition dramatically improved!

I have learned many lessons from this, but the biggest lesson is the importance of praising God! I now understand that thanking God and praising God are two different things. Thanking God, I believe, is acknowledgment of something he has done. Praise, I feel, is acknowledgment of who he is and complete adoration of his awesome grace, mercy, and power.

I certainly continue to thank God throughout the day for all the blessings he bestows upon my family, my friends, and me, but I now also give him praise as I quietly worship him. My son was miraculously healed! For that and so much more, I give God the praise, honor, and glory he deserves.

My son's accident taught me so much about praise. Ruth Myers says that "as we pray and praise God, we free Him to reveal His power as well as His presence. Prayer has been called 'the slender nerve that moves the mighty hand of God' (source unknown). Any form of sincere, believing prayer directs God's power into our lives and situation, but this is especially true of prayer blended with praise. Through praise we focus our attention on God. We acknowledge Him as our source of overcoming power. Praise can flip the switch that turns on the mighty glorious presence of God and tunes us in to His sufficiency. Our lives become a stage on which He reveals Himself in love and power, blessing both us and the people God has placed in our lives."

Buddy Melton relaxes with his fiddle on his farm not far from where he was seriously injured.

We Waited and We Waited

*T*he second incident that I know of Jesus appearing to someone occurred in 1977 and involved one of Buddy's best friends, David Stovall. Listen as David's mother, Tina, tells the story:

We were a busy young family. My husband, John, worked long hours; I was in graduate school. Our children Julie, age ten, and David, age eight, were busy with school and sports. By most standards, our lives were uneventful until one day when I took David to see the pediatrician.

David had complained of headaches now and again, but they never seemed to interfere with his activities. Just the week before our doctor's visit he had complained of a headache and nausea. On the day of our appointment, he actually threw up, and his headache did not go away.

After examining David and hearing about his past complaints of headache and nausea, the doctor sent us immediately to the emergency room to meet a neurosurgeon. Before we left the doctor's office, he prayed with me. I called my husband and my Bible study group and asked for prayer. My husband met me in the emergency room where the neurosurgeon examined David and ordered a brain scan. We anxiously waited for the results.

When the news finally came, it was not what we wanted to hear. "I believe David has a brain tumor" the doctor told us. "And if he does have a tumor, it is inoperable," the doctor went on. "There is definitely fluid on the brain that we must remove because it is causing pressure – thus the headaches, nausea, and vomiting. We can do this by inserting a shunt from David's brain to his stomach. We need to admit David, begin giving him antibiotics, and schedule the surgery for day after tomorrow."

Our world stood still.

After the grandparents arrived my husband and I went immediately to the hospital chapel. There we thanked God for the eight and one-half years we had been blessed to have been David's parents. We knew that he had been loaned to us, and we gave David to God. He was truly in God's hands, and we trusted him for the outcome. It was the very first time that I truly understood Abraham's faith as he stood over his son Isaac trusting God with his fate.

The night before surgery, the doctor explained what the surgery would entail. When he asked if I had any questions, I asked him if he was a Christian. His reply was, "Yes". I then asked him to commit the surgery to God. That night as I was reading my Bible, I asked God to give me a verse to hang onto. I was reading the Psalms and my eyes immediately fell upon Psalm 27:14 LB, "Don't be impatient. Wait for the Lord, and he will come and save you! Be brave, stouthearted and courageous. Yes, wait and he will help you." God knew there would be much waiting ahead of us.

After the surgery the next morning, David was brought back to the room. The doctor told us that because of David's age and size it would be impossible to give him enough medication to alleviate the pain. When he regained consciousness and began to cry, "Mommy, make it stop hurting" all I could do was utter the scripture verse, "I will lift up my eyes unto the hills, from whence cometh my help. My help cometh from the Lord, which made heaven and earth" (Psalm 121:1-2 KJV). I just kept saying this verse over and over in my head.

My sister and brother were with us at the time. When David's cries became more than they could bear, they went down to the chapel to pray. Their prayer was that God would just let David go to sleep. When they returned to the room, they found a peaceful sleeping child. My sister's devotional the day before was from 2 Kings 4:8-37, where Elisha breathed life back into the young boy who had died after complaining of a headache. She knew God would breathe life back into David.

The neurosurgeon recommended that we send the films of David's brain scan to Forsyth Hospital in Winston Salem for another opinion. Due to the location of the mass, it was impossible to biopsy and difficult for the doctors to know what needed to be done next. The pressure in David's brain was alleviated, but the mass was still there.

We waited for more than two months to hear from the doctor at Forsyth.

When the report finally came back, it stated that the doctors believed there was evidence of a brain tumor, but they still questioned what course to follow for treatment.

David was again admitted to the hospital and more tests were run. As a result of these tests, he was referred to a pediatric neurosurgeon at Egleston's Children's Hospital in Atlanta.

We waited for more than a month for an appointment.

When David was finally examined by the doctor in Atlanta and more tests were done, the doctor told us he believed David did have a tumor and that it had grown. He recommended radiation, but his prognosis was grim. He believed that David would go blind, lose movement on his left side, and eventually become a vegetable.

The hospital social worker in Atlanta told us that we needed to tell David that he was dying. We told her that only God knew that, and we trusted him. Soon, nurses from all over the hospital were coming by our room to tell us that they were praying for our son, and that many prayer groups were praying as well. When I asked how they knew we were Christians, one nurse quietly said,

"The social worker noted on David's chart that his mother was a religious fanatic." Thank you, God, for fanatic believers in the power of prayer!

On the way home from Atlanta, we stopped by John's parents' house where we spent the night. Their guest room had two double beds. David and Julie always slept there. That night David went right to sleep, but, as usual, it took Julie much longer. About thirty minutes after the children were put to bed, we heard Julie cry "Mama, Mama!" John and I ran as fast as we could to the room, our hearts in our throats, thinking that something could be wrong with David.

When we got to the bedroom, Julie met us at the door wide-eyed. "Mama," she exclaimed, "a bright light came on in the room, but it was a different kind of light. Jesus was standing beside David's bed. He put his hands on David's head, and he told me that David was going to be all right! I wasn't dreaming, Mama! Do you believe me? Do you believe me, Mama?" She gazed up at us, with anxiety, hope, and joy in her eyes.

We reassured her, "Yes, honey, we believe you." From that moment on, our daughter knew her brother was going to be all right. When our faith was weak, hers was strong.

We had told the doctor in Atlanta that we would like a second opinion before beginning radiation. The doctor recommended that the test results be sent to a hospital in Toronto, Canada. We agreed because they had a pediatric neuroradiologist who was reputed to be the best at reading and interpreting all the tests. "Because of the location of the tumor," the doctors told us, "if it grows, David's condition will be terminal."

We waited to hear from the doctors for the next five weeks.

We waited, and waited. When no word came, we called and were told that the test results and films had been misplaced. We were also told that the doctor was on vacation. By now I think we would have been frantic if it had not been for the verse from Psalms that God had given me at the beginning of this ordeal.

When we finally heard from the neuroradiologist in Canada, we were told that David did indeed have a tumor. It was the recommendation of this doctor that David should receive radiation treatments.

David's neurosurgeon made an appointment at Bowman Gray Hospital in Winston Salem to discuss the option of radiation. We requested that the films and reports be sent to David's neurosurgeon so that he could study them before we took David to Bowman Gray.

We waited to receive the films from Canada. We had to reschedule the appointment three times, and still we waited.

Finally, the films arrived, and we were able to talk to the radiologist and a neurosurgeon at Bowman Gray. They recognized how reluctant we were to start radiation due to the risk of side effects for our child. Trusting God's word to us that we should wait, we waited. We went back to

David's neurosurgeon. He did more tests and sent the results back to Bowman Gray.

We waited once more as those films were lost for two months.

Finally, the doctors at Bowman Gray reviewed both tests and still advised radiation as did three other doctors. A friend of my husband told us about a doctor at Washington's Children's Hospital who had written books on situations similar to David's. We sent all the films and reports to him.

We waited for two months to hear from that doctor.

When enough time had passed and we had heard nothing, we called. "We're so sorry," was the response. "The doctor has moved his office, and his letter giving you his recommendations has been misplaced." This doctor was the only doctor to agree with David's neurosurgeon to wait.

We returned to David's neurosurgeon once again for advice. "Let's continue to wait. If it is a malignant tumor, it will be non-curable and eventually fatal. We have nothing to lose by waiting to see if it grows."

Six months later, David had another brain scan, but we had to wait for the results because the doctor was out of town. One day as I watched David playing outside, I suddenly realized tears were rolling down my face. My wise daughter, now eleven years old, asked, "Mama why are you crying? Don't you know God told us that David is going to be all right?"

When the doctor finally called a couple of weeks later, he told us that there had been a definite change in David's scan. He felt the shunt was going to take care of the problem. "As David grows, his shunt will need to be revised from time to time," he said. "But for now let's just wait." Brain scans were continued on a regular basis.

Six years later, as we continued to wait, David's neurosurgeon referred us to a doctor in Charlotte for an NMR (now known as an MRI) which was still in experimental stages. This doctor felt that the tumor was growing and was terminal. This information was given in David's presence. David was quiet on our three-hour ride home. When we arrived home, David simply stated, "If God wants to heal me he can, and if he doesn't that is okay, too." At the age of 14, David, too, had just said, "God, I am in your hands."

Waiting is something neither my husband nor I do very well. But because we had turned to the Lord in the very beginning of this ordeal and had depended on his guidance, we were able to stay strong and not go absolutely crazy with the uncertainty, and with the frustration we had to endure dealing with this overwhelming situation.

I know that if God had not given us that scripture verse in the very beginning we would probably have made a terrible mistake by following the unanimous advice of four different doctors. We did not choose radiation with its unknown side effects. Instead we were able to wait patiently depending on God to help us as he had promised to do. He had told us to be brave, stouthearted, and courageous and to WAIT.

After thirty-five years, many shunt revisions and much waiting, our son is a normal healthy young man. Let us all praise God for such a miracle!

Let us also praise God for his written word, the Bible. God first communicated with David's family through Scripture, giving them hope and guidance that would help sustain them through his illness. Reliance on God's Word kept them going during their long ordeal. In this inspired book, we are able to hear God's voice and be led by his spirit. We are so blessed that he chose to communicate with us in such a clear, and for many of us, accessible way. As we read his word and listen for his voice, he will lead, guide, and direct us in our daily lives and enable us to develop a deeper faith and confidence.

Oswald Chambers, in his book *My Utmost for His Highest*, says, "When God gives you a vision and darkness follows, wait. God will bring the vision He has given you to reality in your life if you will wait on His timing. Never try to help God fulfill His word. He is Almighty God, El-Shaddai, the All-Powerful God."

*David with his sister Julie shortly after
his brain tumor was discovered.*

Jesus Appeared

*I*know of another incident in which Jesus appeared to someone, and once again that individual is a female. This incident concerns, Linda, a deeply spiritual woman whose son was attending summer school out of town to make up some class credits. He needed these credits in order to be promoted to the next grade. The week before his finals, he had been with some others who had gotten into trouble. He was in jeopardy of being kicked out of summer school which would mean that he would not finish and thus not be promoted to the next grade in the fall. She shares, "During this time of uncertainty, I prayed for hours at a time it seemed. When I looked up from praying late one evening, I saw Jesus sitting near me. He was dressed in white, and though I neither saw his face nor heard his voice, I was comforted by knowing that he was sitting there peacefully with me. I seemed to know that whatever the outcome, he would be with me. As it turned out, my son was able to take the finals, pass, and in the fall return to high school in the next grade."

Continuing, she says, "I will never forget how his presence made me feel. I was alone, and I had no one to talk with about this situation – no one except my Lord. After that experience, I knew that no matter what, I would never be truly alone. No matter what, Jesus would always be there for me. Certainly I had always been taught this lesson but being told something and experiencing it firsthand is very different."

For some reason, in each of these accounts, Jesus has appeared to a woman: my daughter-in-law Carla, David's sister Julie, and my friend praying for her son. I am not sure why this is, but I have thought a great deal about all three.

It is interesting that the first person Jesus appeared to after his resurrection was a woman by the name of Mary Magdalene. I think one reason that he appeared to her first was because she was so sad; her sorrow was so great! He wanted to comfort her. He wanted to reassure her. I believe that those are the same reasons he appeared to the three women I just mentioned. Certainly he could have healed Buddy and David and helped my friend's son without making his presence known. However, by appearing to Carla, Julie, and Linda, he was not only giving them complete assurance that their loved ones were going to be fine, but he was also strengthening their faith. I believe Christ has a soft spot in his heart for women, probably because of his love for his mother.

Touched by Jesus

*T*his beautiful story is also told by my friend, Linda Minor:

Not long after my husband left me and I was living alone, I had gone to bed early as I often did in those days. I would lie in bed for long periods of time, sometimes crying and sometimes praying. I kept trying to make sense of my life and consider my future. One night as I was lying in bed crying and praying a quiet stillness filled the room and a peace fell upon me. It was in that quiet moment that I felt God's warm hand gently patting me on the back. I distantly heard him softly say, "It'll be okay, it'll be okay."

That same peace is with me today twenty-three years later. As life continues to be life, with its uncertainties, hardships, disappointments, and heartaches, very clearly I remember his comforting hand patting my back and his reassuring words spoken into my ear. I am reminded, yet again, that "It Is Well With My Soul", no matter the circumstances.

Throughout my life I have learned so much about prayer. I have learned that prayer is not about fancy words. Prayer is a private conversation with my Lord and Savior. Prayer keeps me centered. It touches my life and those for whom I pray. It allows me to see many everyday miracles more readily, and it helps me see Christ in all peoples and in this, his creation. Prayer helps me through uncertain and confusing times. It gives me comfort. Prayer is peace.

Rescued by an Angel

The Bible tells us, that God also sends help in the form of guardian angels. Psalm 91:11 LB says, "For he orders his angels to protect you wherever you go." What a blessing it is to have a heavenly father who loves us so dearly!

Billy Graham, in his book, *Angels: God's Secret Agents*, tells us, "God has provided Christians with both offensive and defensive weapons. We are not to be fearful; we are not to be distressed; we are not to be intimidated. The Bible, in nearly three hundred different places, teaches that God has countless angels at His command. God has commissioned these angels to aid His children in their struggles against Satan. I am convinced that these heavenly beings exist and that they provide unseen aid on our behalf. It seems that angels have the ability to change their appearance and shuttle in a flash from heaven to earth and back again."

Following is a wonderful story told by Lorraine Lee, the mother of Linda Minor. She and her husband, Dr. William R. Lee, served as volunteer medical missionaries worldwide for over forty years. Here is her story in her own words:

> In the mid-1990s, my husband, Billy, and I
> were preparing for a mission trip to Russia and

China with friends, Dr. and Mrs. Carter Dobbs. Dr. Dobbs was a dentist and was going to provide dental care for the people in the two countries. Before leaving the states we had received a call from a mission agent requesting us to be couriers of forty thousand dollars to Russia. We readily agreed. The money was to be in new one hundred dollar bills. We decided that it would be wise for us to divide the money and carry it in a special money belt under our clothes. Needless to say, we felt very uneasy being responsible for this much money.

As we were approaching South Korea for a flight connection, our feelings of uneasiness were magnified by the unrest in the country. Our president, Jimmy Carter, had worked diligently to mediate tensions between the United States, Russia, and North, and South Korea. Because of this, there was much unrest in South Korea and a great deal of animosity toward Americans.

We were in South Korea for thirty-six hours. During this time we saw no other Americans at the hotel or in other areas that we visited. Throughout the city there were demonstrations against the United States.

The next day we arrived at the airport early. We went through the first check point without a problem, and our luggage passed the second security. However, when a Korean lady with a security wand checked and frisked me, she found the bulky money belt that I was wearing.

In her broken English she asked what it was that she was feeling, and I explained that it was my money. She immediately pushed me over to an area behind a curtain and wanted to see it. I cooperated with her request. When she saw the money, she immediately had me lay it all on a table in view of every one, and she called her superiors. Three or four men arrived quickly and immediately began questioning me.

"What are you doing with that much money?" they asked. "Where are your papers? How much money do you have?"

My fearful and trembling response to their questions went something like this: "Papers? What papers?" Then I started searching frantically through my purse pulling out all kinds of official papers; none of them were what they wanted. Trying to act innocent, I asked if I needed to fill out a paper.

They said, "No! No! You should have one!"

I said over and over that I didn't understand. Again and again I asked, "What's the problem?"

As the four men and one woman were fingering and tossing the twenty thousand dollars, I pointed to my husband and Dr. and Mrs. Dobbs who had made it through the security check and explained that we were making a long trip to Russia, Hong Kong, and China and that we needed this much money. I offered to show them my tickets. They were not interested.

They wanted to know how much money was there. I shrugged my shoulders and said, "Oh, about twenty," deliberating leaving off the thousand, noticing they were not counting.

I was getting more nervous as time went on. I feared that the money would be confiscated and that I would be put in a Korean prison. At this point my husband realized the seriousness of the situation, and he and the Dobbs' began to pray.

Suddenly, a man appeared wearing a black suit, white shirt, and black tie. He took command and said to me in perfect English, "Where have you been? You are late! The plane is leaving you! Get your things and come with me." I gathered the money quickly without looking at the lady or her superiors. He got me by the arm and said, "Hurry!" He told the people in line at the passport check that I was missing my plane, and he put me ahead of them and through the checkpoint. He took my husband and the Dobbs' through another line.

As I was hurrying to the gate, I looked back to thank the man, but he was gone. I never saw him again. We arrived at the final gate an hour before the plane was scheduled to depart for Russia. It was then that the questions came to our minds: How did this man know which plane and the time of our flight? How did he just disappear?

We know the answer to these questions. We believe the Lord intervened in this near catastrophic event by sending a guardian angel in the form of a man in a black suit. None of us recall his facial features.

What a beautiful illustration of God's love and protection! The Bible tells us in Hebrews 1:14 KJV that angels are "ministering spirits, sent forth to minister for them who shall be heirs of salvation."

Dr. and Mrs. William R. Lee in old Russian tank

God Has Already Answered

Sometimes, friends are like earthly angels, there to help us in our times of need. This is a story about just such an individual.

Tina and John Stovall have always depended on God to meet their every need. Both are deeply spiritual individuals who strongly believe in the power of prayer. I have shared the story of their son David's healing from a brain tumor. The following is a wonderful event that occurred during their ordeal dealing with their son's tumor, again recounted from Tina's perspective:

> When we decided to get a second opinion about David's condition from the professionals in Atlanta, we knew that we would probably be there for three or four days while David was assessed. The problem was that we did not have enough money to cover the expenses for such a trip. We felt that we were going to be a hundred dollars short.
>
> As a young couple with two small children, times were tough. I was in graduate school and was not working. John got paid only once a month so it was going to be a couple of weeks before he got

a check. We had a savings account at the bank, but if we took any money out of that account, we would be penalized. However, we decided to call the bank and just see how much the penalty would be. When I called, I was told that everyone was busy but that someone would call me back. Moments later the phone rang and a voice said, "Go check your mailbox."

With a bit of fear I walked down to the mailbox and looked inside. There was a card which read, "God has laid it on my heart to share with you." Inside the card was a hundred dollar bill!

Crying and praising God, I walked back up the driveway. When I got back to the house, the phone was ringing. It was the bank. "You called for help?" the lady asked.

"I did," I replied, "but God has already answered!"

Once again God had been there for us. He had told us through his Word in Psalm 27:14 that we were to wait for him and that he would come and help us. On this day and many other days to come, he did just that. With love he was teaching us patience as we learned to wait. With love he was teaching us faith as we waited for his guidance. With love he was teaching us courage as we struggled to remain calm in the storm of our sick child's life. Looking back on those terrible months of uncertainty, I can see that through it all God was there!

When You Pray and Get No Answer, Try Laying Down Fleece

My husband, Frank, worked as a mortician/funeral director at a funeral home in Asheville, North Carolina. Such positions didn't pay very well, but because he felt that God had called him to this profession, he wanted to continue to work in this field. However, he wanted to somehow supplement his income and had been searching for a way to do this.

One evening he came home from work and upon entering the house exclaimed with excitement in his voice, "I've found some property that I think we should buy! It has a little house on it that would be perfect as a rental. I believe it would be a wise investment!"

"But in order to do this, I would have to go back to work," I told him. Then gently I reminded him that when our first child was born, we had decided that I would stay home and not return to work until the youngest child started school. "We knew that to do this, we would have to sacrifice a great deal, but we felt that the sacrifice would be worth it. Have you changed your mind about this commitment?" I asked.

After further discussion, we knew that we now had to decide

if we were to going to stay the course or change our plans. We decided to pray about the decision trusting God to lead us. Days went by and neither of us felt that we could determine God's direction.

When I was growing up, my grandmother would always "lay down fleece" when she had to make a decision that would have changed not only her life but the lives of her family.

In the sixth chapter of Judges, it tells us that the Israelites had been suffering under the oppression of the Midianites for seven years. Then an angel of the Lord appeared to a young man by the name of Gideon and told him that he was to lead his people against the Midianites. When Gideon heard these words he protested, "Sir, how can I save Israel? My family is the poorest in the whole tribe of Manasseh, and I am the least thought of in the entire family!" (Judges 6:15 LB). I'm sure he probably thought that God had made a mistake in calling him. He probably also worried that no one would follow the likes of him into battle.

When the Lord heard Gideon's concerns, he promised him that he would be with him and that he would quickly destroy the Midianites. At that Gideon replied, "If it is really true that you are going to help me like that, then give me a miracle to prove it!" (Judges 6:17 LB). God answered Gideon's request and performed a miracle and Gideon believed. Fighting forces throughout the tribes of Manasseh, Asher, Zebulun, and Naphtali were summoned, and together they prepared to fight the Midianites. Before Gideon led the men into battle, he said to God, "If you are really going to use me to save Israel as you promised, prove it to me this way: I'll put some wool on the threshing floor tonight, and if, in the morning, the fleece is wet and the ground is dry, I will know you are going to help me!" (Judges 6:36-37 LB).

The next morning when Gideon awoke and felt the fleece not only was it wet, but he was able to wring out a whole bowlful of water! How much more clear could God be? But still (like many of us) Gideon worried so again he called out to God. "Please don't be angry with me, but let me make one more test: this time let the fleece remain dry while the ground around it is wet" (Judges 6:39 LB).

The next morning Gideon discovered that the fleece was dry but that the ground around it was covered with dew! So, in the face of overwhelming evidence, Gideon believed.

Then God told Gideon that there were too many men in his army. If all of them went out to fight the Midianites, the people of Israel would boast that they had saved themselves by their own strength. God was asking the Israelites to trust in his strength and not theirs. "Send home any of your men who are timid and frightened," (Judges 7:3 LB) God told Gideon. So in the end twenty-two thousand men left and only ten thousand remained.

But God said that was still too many! He told Gideon to send the men to the spring, and he would tell Gideon which men were to remain. When the men drank from the spring, three hundred cupped the water in their hands to get it to their mouths. All the others, the vast majority, lapped up the water like dogs with their mouths in the stream. God told Gideon that He would conquer the Midianites with only the three hundred men who drank from cupped hands and that is exactly what He did.

Frank and I now needed clear direction. There was too much at stake to risk making a mistake. In Proverbs 3:5-6 NIV it says: "Trust in the Lord with all your heart, and lean not on your own understanding; in all your ways acknowledge him, and he will make your paths straight."

We knew that only God could see the future, so we needed to lean on his understanding. He has promised that if we will allow him to have complete control that he will direct our paths.

I had never laid down fleece, but because our decision had the potential to impact our family for years to come, I now decided to do just that. That day, Frank and I had worked in the yard most of the day. During that time, Frank had wanted to cut down some irises that I had planted two or three years before. They had never bloomed, and Frank saw no need to keep them. "Let's leave them," I begged, "and give them a little more time."

That night while reading my Bible, Psalm 5:1-3, 8 LB said: "O Lord, hear me praying; listen to my plea, O God my King, for I will never pray to anyone but you. Each morning I will look to you in heaven and lay my requests before you, praying earnestly... Lord, lead me as you promised me you would;... Tell me clearly what to do, which way to turn."

Later that night as I was saying my evening prayers, I told God that because we had been unable to discern his direction in regard to purchasing the property that I was going to lay down fleece. "God," I prayed, "if we are *not* supposed to purchase the property, let one of those irises be blooming in the morning. If we are supposed to purchase the property, please let the irises be just as they were today, with no blooms at all."

The next morning I awoke about six o'clock. I could not wait to get outside and have a look at those irises. Putting on my robe and tennis shoes, I ran outside. There, before me, stood a lovely purple iris in full bloom where there had been only leaves the day before! Needless to say, we did not purchase the property.

I can think of one other time that I laid down fleece. This instance occurred many years later. After earning an advanced degree, I was unprepared for the doors that opened for me. The job opportunities were varied and wonderful and each one meant that I would be working with a very different group of people. I finally narrowed the jobs to three. On one I would be working with young people that had chosen teaching as a profession. On another I would be helping teachers who had chosen to work with gifted and talented students. On the third I would be doing consulting work in the area of language arts. I had no idea which one I should take or on which one I could do the most good. I prayed and prayed about my choices but never really felt that God was telling me that any one was the job I should take. Therefore, once again, I decided to lay down fleece. On the morning I decided to do this, I was driving to Raleigh for a meeting. In order to arrive at the meeting by 9:00 A.M., I had to leave home at 5:00 A.M. I knew that one of the women who would also be attending the meeting would be getting up about 7:00 A.M. and leaving home about 8:15. So about 7:00, I prayed that if I was supposed to take job #1, she would wear predominately red; if I should take job #2, she would wear predominately white; and if I should take job #3, she would wear predominately blue.

I couldn't wait to get to the meeting to see what she was wearing. When I arrived, she was nowhere to be found. In fact, she came in late. As soon as I could, I made my way over to where she was seated, and the first thing out of my mouth was, "Is that what you planned to wear today?"

With a disturbed look on her face she replied, "Is something wrong with my outfit?"

"Oh, no, you look great, and I will explain why I asked in a moment," I said hurriedly, "but right now I just need to know if this is what you had originally planned to wear today."

"Actually it isn't," she replied with a very puzzled look on her face. "I had planned to wear a green dress, but when I got up, I suddenly changed my mind and felt I should wear this. Now, I really must know why you asked."

Quickly I told her about my morning prayer, and together we had a good laugh. She was wearing a white blouse, navy skirt, and a red blazer! "Now what do you think God means by this?" I asked.

"Well, I don't know," she replied, "but I certainly think he has a sense of humor!"

When I got home, I met with my pastor who said he felt that God was saying, "Choose any of the three jobs that you want. I will be fine with any of them." I made my choice, and in the end found out that it really did not matter which I had chosen because I wasn't in that job very long. God had bigger plans for me.

When You Seek God's Will, You Will Be Successful

*B*eginning in 1 Samuel 16:1, you can read about the life of David. In 1 Samuel 18:14 LB it says, "David continued to succeed in everything he undertook for the Lord was with him." One reason for David's constant success was because he continually sought God's will. For example, in 2 Samuel 5:19 LB, David asked the Lord if he should fight against the Philistines and if God was going to defeat them for him. The Lord replied, "Yes, go ahead, for I will give them to you."

From childhood, my husband Frank and I had heard Bible stories of biblical characters like David and were taught the importance of always seeking God's will. Therefore, it was completely natural for us to seek his will for our business and career decisions as well as other aspects of our lives.

Less than a year after we decided not to purchase the rental property that would have forced me to return to the workplace, Frank heard of a business that was for sale only three blocks from our house. It was a flower shop, and the price was such that we could manage to buy it without my returning to work. Once again, we prayed about the decision and felt that God was leading us to buy the business, which we did.

.

That first year the business grew so much, we had to move it to a much larger location. My husband purchased an old service station directly across from the V. A Hospital in Oteen, North Carolina, and remodeled it. He transformed it into such a beautiful building that it caught the eye of many folks passing by. Because the location was so wonderful, across the street from the hospital and not far from a funeral home, the business grew even more.

Two years later we opened a second flower shop in Swannanoa, the next town down the road. Both businesses had managers, designers, and deliverymen working long hours as the businesses continued to grow. We had depended on God to lead, guide, and direct us. We had listened and obeyed, and he had blessed us beyond measure!

I Forgot God Loved Him More

*A*nd then came the day when, like David who desperately wanted Bathsheba, we wanted something so badly that we allowed our personal desire to override God's will for our lives.

While we were operating the two flower shops, a friend of Frank's asked him to go into partnership with him and open a funeral home in Weaverville, North Carolina, a small, quaint mountain town north of Asheville. Frank had worked as a licensed mortician/funeral director for twelve years in Asheville, North Carolina. However, it was a lifelong dream to own a funeral home of his own. Because I loved him so much, I too, desperately wanted to see him realize his dream. Since my schooldays, I had been so blessed with Frank's love and support that I wanted to give my encouragement and support to him.

Frank had been there for me since we were in the eighth grade. That year he had taken me to the eighth grade prom and the next day a teacher had asked him who he had taken. His reply was, "I took the girl I'm going to marry." (I did not know that, however, until after we were married when that teacher came through the receiving line after the wedding and told me the story.) From the eighth grade on, Frank and I had dated. Whenever anything bad happened in my life, I only had to turn around and Frank would always be there for me.

Frank & Ann when they were in the ninth grade

Because I was the product of a broken home, a family became most important to me – more important even than job or career. A good marriage was paramount and was always a part of my prayer requests. While in high school I can remember praying every day, "God, please help me to choose the right young man to marry. Please don't let me make a mistake. Please don't let me get this wrong. Please help me to pick the right young man, but please, God, let it be Frank Melton."

I loved Frank more than anyone else loved him, I thought, but what I had forgotten was that God loved him also. In fact, I should have realized that God loved him even more than I did. So, now that Frank and I were contemplating opening a new funeral home, instead of asking God to show me his will for our lives, I completely left him out of the decision.

Neither Frank nor I did what we had always done in the past. We did not pray about the decision. We did not ask God to give us direction and to show us what he wanted. We did not seek his will in the matter. Frank saw the chance to realize a longtime dream of owning his own funeral home, and I saw the chance to be the support for Frank that he had always been for me. We were looking at ourselves, our hopes and dreams, instead of towards God and his will for our lives. And we were both, I believe, afraid that God would say, "No!"

Obviously we had also forgotten God's wonderful promise: "Delight yourself in the Lord, and he will give you the desires of your heart" (Psalm 37:4 NIV).

So instead of waiting for God to tell us when and where to open a funeral home, we sold both of the businesses that we owned at the time and went to Weaverville where we converted an old church into a funeral home.

From the moment we began setting up the new business, anything that could go wrong did so. For example, the owner of the other funeral home in town went to the deacons of the First Baptist Church and tried to get them to stop the sale of their old church building to us. When that failed, they went before the town board and tried to get them to refuse to give us a permit to open the business. And on and on it went. It seemed that every day we were faced with a new dilemma. The final blow came when Frank was in a serious automobile accident. After weeks in the hospital, the doctors felt that he needed surgery and even then might never be able to work again. During this time I was trying to keep the business going while working full time as a teacher in another town. And where was Frank's business partner during this time, you may be wondering. Why was he not helping us? The answer is that his marriage fell apart, and so did he! Frank had been left to shoulder the burden of the new business alone.

Because of the seriousness of Frank's condition, we felt we needed a second opinion and so we made an appointment at Bowman-Gray Hospital in Winston Salem. There the doctors were able to fit him with a brace that made it possible for him to be out of bed and able to walk. In a few weeks, he was able to return home and eventually return to work. By this time, however, the business had gone from bad to worse. We had to close the funeral home and sell the building.

Fortunately, we had rented our house in Asheville during the time we were away and were able to return there. In the weeks that followed, Frank searched for a job. Together we humbled ourselves before our Lord and asked for forgiveness, not once but many times a day, every day. Our shame was as great as our guilt. Our prayers remind me of those found in Psalms 3:3 LB, "But Lord, you are my shield, my glory, and my only hope. You alone can lift my head now bowed in shame."

Fortunately for us, God has promised that if we will humble ourselves, he will care for us, forgive us, show us mercy, and grant us peace.

"Humble yourselves...Casting all your care
upon him; for he careth for you."

1 Peter 5:6-7 KJV

"But all who humble themselves before the Lord shall be
given every blessing, and shall have wonderful peace."

Psalm 37:11 LB

My husband, Frank Melton

We Started Over

*I*n a few months, following Frank's accident and our failure in Weaverville, he accepted a job as manager of a funeral home in Waynesville, and I got a job in the same county teaching third grade at Hazelwood Elementary School. We moved to Waynesville and began to start over.

When I think of the period in our lives just before the move, I am always reminded of Matthew 26: 41 LB, which reads, "Keep alert and pray. Otherwise temptation will overpower you. For the spirit indeed is willing, but how weak the body is!"

That verse will be forever printed on my mind and heart. Those were the words spoken by Christ to Peter, James, and John in the garden of Gethsemane just before he was betrayed. By not seeking his will for our lives, had we not also betrayed Jesus? We had not remained alert – watching out so that Satan could not slip in when we were not looking. We had not kept praying. Temptation had indeed overpowered us. It was a hard lesson indeed, and one we would not soon forget.

Even in our misfortune, God was still at work in our lives bestowing his blessings upon us. Amazingly, we were able to purchase a wonderful old home on the most historic street in

Waynesville. The street is named for the town's founders, the Love family, and was the first residential street in Waynesville. It was the house and neighborhood of my dreams! And even more amazing is the fact that years later I would learn that Robert Love, who founded the town, is my fourth great grandfather. God started us out in this next chapter of our lives with a beautiful home on Love Lane, a visible sign that he keeps his promises and perhaps has a sense of humor as well.

Our new neighborhood was a wonderful place to live. The families were warm and welcoming and the children delightful. The day we moved in we noticed a large group of children and young people sitting in a yard across the street. All were taking turns swinging on a swing fastened to a large oak tree. It wasn't long before they all came over to our house and introduced themselves. They ranged in age from kindergarten to college. They explained that they were going to Maggie Valley to the water slide and wanted to know if our children could go with them. Thus began a wonderful time in our children's lives as well as our own. God had once again blessed us beyond measure!

A lesson that I learned from reading Ruth Myers is "how easy it is to slip into self-sufficiency, to lean on our own wisdom and abilities, our own power and forcefulness. To do so is pride. We all know the saying, 'pride goes before a fall'. The real truth is that by our own abilities and wisdom, we can do nothing of value in God's eyes. Knowing this helps us to yield to Christ and to trust Him." She goes on to say that "our failures and unmet needs are in reality great blessings in disguise. They remind us that we're not qualified to run our own lives. They press us to commit ourselves to Christ and trust in Him. They keep us humble."

Daily I praise God that he promises to cause all things — even things that are contrary to his will — to work together for good for those who love him and who are called according to his purposes (Romans 8:28 NRSV author's paraphrase).

I love the prayer written by Ruth Myers in which she thanks God that "when He, as a refiner of silver, uses painful, fiery trials to bring the scum to the top of our lives, that He also gives us the grace to cooperate with Him in removing that scum instead of just stirring it back in." And she praises him that "He is so full of compassion that the outcome of His purifying work is more than worth all that He lets us go through."

Difficult Decisions

*D*iscerning God's will for your life is not always easy. Sometimes outside forces make it difficult to know what to do. They make it difficult to make right decisions. And to make it even harder, sometimes these outside forces are friends and family who want only the best for you and who feel that the advice they are giving is correct. At these times it is important to delve deeper into God's word, spend more time with him in prayer, and listen for his voice.

Such was the case for me when I was offered a job as an outside evaluator in the Jackson County school system. An outside evaluator is someone who goes into classrooms and observes and evaluates teachers. In some counties, the teachers could choose whether or not they would be evaluated. If they chose to do so, they were paid well for agreeing to be observed. However, in Jackson County, the teachers had no choice in the matter. They were *told* that they would be evaluated, and they would receive no extra pay for their trouble. As an evaluator, my visit would be unannounced, and I would spend one hour writing down everything the teacher said and did, as well as much of what the students said or did. This information was subsequently compiled, studied and rated. The teacher, principal, and central office received a copy of the evaluation.

While this job was a good professional opportunity, I had reservations about accepting it. What concerned me most about the process was that at no time during the observation could the evaluator share an idea or provide help, insight, or encouragement. As an educator, I had been trained to provide help and encouragement whenever and wherever I felt it was needed. This forced detachment went against the grain. I simply knew that I could not do this job. I could not sit still for an hour and just observe and write. I knew I would find myself in a classroom where the teacher was struggling with a difficult situation. To live with myself, I would just have to step forward and say, "Have you thought of doing that this way?" or "I once saw this done and it worked beautifully. Would you allow me to demonstrate?" or "What if you tried this?" or "I would love to help you if you would allow me to do so."

However, the position carried a great deal of prestige, not to mention a healthy paycheck, and so I was encouraged by everyone to take the job. The more they encouraged, the harder I prayed, and the more I felt God telling me not to take the job. The school superintendent in Haywood County where I worked even called my husband and told him that I was crazy if I did not take the job! Now, even if you are fairly stable, something like that can drive you crazy! As an added incentive, the superintendent in Jackson County also promised me a job at their central office if things did not work out with the outside evaluator program.

I don't know that I have ever prayed longer or harder about a decision. After each prayer time with the Lord concerning this job opportunity, I felt strongly that it was not God's will for me. So, in the end I did not take the job.

Only one year after the outside evaluator program began in

Jackson County, it ended. Those who had sold their homes and moved to the county to direct the program had to start over again somewhere else. The superintendent who had offered me a job at the central office if the program folded was no longer there.

As for me, however, shortly after I turned down the job, I received word that I had received a full scholarship that would completely pay for my doctoral program. What I did not know at the time was that while I was not going to Jackson County now, I would be going in the future, and when I got there, I would be able to help teachers in ways that I would not have been able to as an evaluator. I could even say, "How about if we team teach and figure out how to correct this situation together?" I would eventually go to Jackson County, and there God would teach me everything I would need to be successful in my next two jobs.

Working Their Way Home on God's Plan

Jobs and money, along with illness, death, and relationships are some of our greatest challenges. But as a Christian we have a wonderful helper in the Lord to lead, guide, and direct us. If we will only depend on him, he will direct us to the place we need to be. Following is my retelling of a wonderful story about a couple who truly depend on the Lord to meet their every need.

This couple was having a difficult time. The husband had lost his job when the company he worked for downsized. For many months he searched for employment. To make it through this difficult time, the couple cashed in their 401K and used all of their retirement to make ends meet. Finally, he was able to get a job at a bank in Canada. While he was told that the job was for only six months, he felt that if he worked hard enough and did a really good job he might be hired full time. The wife quit her job in the states and traveled with her husband to Canada thinking that this would be their new home.

After working extra hours and weekends, he reported to his boss that he had completed his assignment three months early.

Instead of being praised for his efforts, he was told that he had worked himself out of a job!

Now the couple did what they always did, they depended on God to give them direction in this difficult situation. They got their dry erase board and a pen, and they made two lists. The first list named the commands of God such as forgive, obey, love, give, pray, listen, follow, believe, and seek. The second list named the promises of God such as love, joy, peace, life, and prosperity.

After creating the two lists, they lay down on the floor prostrate before the Lord, and holding hands, they prayed for God to help them. After praying, the wife got on the internet and began searching for job opportunities for her husband. Since the couple had gotten married and moved away, she had longed to return home – to the area where she grew up. As she searched the internet, there appeared an ad for a job in Sylva only twenty miles from her birthplace. She couldn't believe it!

Calling for her husband, she said, "Please get on the phone right now and apply for this job! I have no idea if you are qualified or can even do the job, but you have to try!" He called and was told that they wanted to meet with him that week! Quickly the couple packed their belongings and began the eighteen hour drive to Sylva. The interview not only went well but was followed by a job offer!

Now the wife realized that she, too, needed to look for employment. She purchased a copy of the local newspaper, *The Sylva Herald*, and there was an advertisement for a position as a church secretary. She called, got an interview, and was offered the job. The amazing thing was that the ad was supposed to have been removed from the newspaper the week before! God had met both their needs. He had provided a job for each of them in the area in which they longed to live. They had depended on the Lord to take care of them, and he had done just that.

In John 15:7 NRSV it says, "If you abide in me, and my words abide in you, ask whatever you wish, and it shall be done for you." Concerning this passage, Andrew Murray wrote, "Our acceptance with God and our access to Him is through Christ. As we consciously abide in Him, we are free from the power of our old nature. In this divine freedom from self-will, we are free to ask God for what we want, being influenced now by our new nature. And God will do it. Let us treasure this place of freedom through abiding in Christ — and believe that our requests right now are heard and will be answered."

Wet but Wiser

*I*n the book of Jonah, we learn that when God told Jonah to go to Nineveh, Jonah disobeyed and was swallowed by a whale. After three days the whale spit him out on the shore, a wet, soggy mess.

On this day I was about to follow suit, sloshing in Jonah's footsteps. The school where I worked had gotten out early for Christmas. Several of my friends and I had gathered at a friend's home in Canton to have lunch and exchange gifts. About three o'clock the party ended, and I got in my car and began my drive home. It was very cold. The rain was pouring down my windshield, my defroster was working overtime, and I just wanted to get home the quickest way possible. When I got to the stop sign at the end of the street, a voice said, "Turn left and go through Bethel." The message was so clear that I immediately replied out loud, "Bethel? Why would I want to go through Bethel?"

And so I turned right and drove toward home thinking, "To have gone through Bethel would have been so much further, and the road is so curvy. I'm glad I used my better judgment this time." Congratulating myself on a good decision, I cautiously drove on. I had not gone more than five or six miles when suddenly the tail lights of the car in front of me flashed a streaky red warning across my windshield. Even though I reacted quickly and applied my brakes, the road was wet and slick, and I found myself in a ten-car pileup with my bumper locked well into the bumper of the car in front of me!

Needless to say I spent the remainder of the afternoon, along with many other drivers, commiserating in the cold and wet, and talking to highway patrolmen, wrecker service attendants, and insurance agents. I, like Jonah, was a wet soggy mess. According to the mechanics, my car was a total loss. What was not a loss was God's lesson for me. My Heavenly Father had been trying to protect me – to tell me what was in my best interests. God's better judgment would have brought me home safe and dry, hours earlier, and thousands of dollars cheaper. That day I vowed that I would never again fail to heed God's voice. I might argue, but I would not disobey. Little did I know a few years later God would be put me to the test again!

Tested Again

*T*wo years after totaling my car on a rainy stretch of road because I had not listened to God and obeyed him, I was put to the test again. After my accident I had vowed that I would never again disobey God, no matter what he asked me to do. Now, as I was driving to work and talking to God, he told me that my husband and I were to open a funeral home in Sylva, our hometown

The message was so clear that when I arrived at work I told a good friend of mine, with whom I had grown up, just what God had told me. She worked part time as a realtor, and I asked her if she would be willing to spend one day looking for a place to start such a business. She agreed.

When my husband, Frank, got home from work that evening, I waited to tell him what God had told me, holding my tongue, until I knew I had his undivided attention. Despite my caution, his reaction was still a bit more than I had expected. "Are you serious?" he stormed. "We could lose everything we have worked for the past twenty-six years." Still cautious after the Weaverville debacle, Frank was hesitant to think about taking another huge business risk.

"You know," I replied testily, "I'm just the messenger here. I'm just telling you what God told me. You pray about it for a week or so and see what God tells you!"

I could certainly understand Frank's hesitation and uncertainty. We had experienced failure in the past, and now I was suggesting that we risk that again. This time, however, the business had not been our idea, but God's. We had failed in the past because we had not sought God's will for our lives. This time God was clearly telling us what he wanted us to do.

A week later Frank came to me. "I've prayed long and hard about this," he said, "and I feel that we should do what God told us to do."

When Frank's boss learned that we were going to open a funeral home in Sylva, he came to the house to talk with us. He was very concerned. Did we, he wanted to know, understand the problems we would surely face? Did we understand the risks? "We do understand," we assured him, "but we have God on our side. Romans 8:31 KJV says, 'If God be for us, who can be against us? ' "

"We know that there will be people who will oppose what we are trying to do," we told him. "But God is certainly more powerful than any force that may come against us, and he obviously has plans for us."

We found a building. A few days later Frank and our daughter, Myra, sat at the dining room table. As Frank explained his vision for the funeral home, Myra drew the floor plan for the business. Together they designed the exterior of the building and the floor plan for the interior. A builder was selected, and the work got under way.

While the building was progressing, we were busy looking for pews for the chapel and the necessary rolling stock. "Rolling stock" refers to the family car, hearse, flower truck, and other vehicles necessary for a funeral home. There was only one problem. We could find no pews or rolling stock we could afford! When we had decided to honor God's command, we reminded him that we had no money to begin such a business — not that he did not already know this. He did. Before we had begun the funeral home, we had only our home and a small savings account for the education of our two children who were in college. Now the bank owned the house. We were truly operating in God's hands.

We had traveled far and wide to find pews and rolling stock, but in every case we had come up empty-handed. "Well," I said, "we have certainly tried. Now we must give our list to the Lord and trust him to find what we need. We'll just claim God's promise in Psalm 9:10 LB, 'All those who know your mercy, Lord, will count on you for help. For you have never yet forsaken those who trust in you.' "

A few days later we stopped at a funeral home where Frank had worked several years before just to visit with the men he had worked with. During our conversation, Frank happened to mention that he was trying to find rolling stock. "We might just have what you need," his friend replied. Together they went out back to the garages to look. "We have just recently upgraded our rolling stock. These vehicles are for sale if you're interested," his friend added.

"What are you asking for them?" Frank wanted to know.

"Not much. We've had them for several years."

When we left there, we were the thankful owners of vehicles that were not only the color we had hoped to purchase but in almost new condition and at a price far below what we had planned to pay. A few days later we found pews that were also within our price range. We had asked God for help, and he had provided.

We used the furniture we had in our home to furnish the inside of the funeral home. We went to a discount fabric store and purchased fabric so that our two couches, love seat and ten chairs would match. Then, thanks to the kindness of a good friend at the local community college, we reupholstered all thirteen pieces in four days! If you have ever reupholstered just one piece, you will certainly know that we were only able to redo thirteen pieces in such a short time with divine help.

With the help of family and friends, the day came when we were ready to open for business. We planned an open house for the public on a Sunday afternoon, but before that we held a private service to dedicate the business to God.

We had come to this town to serve the people. It was our prayer that we would be a blessing to them and to God. As I sat there listening to the preacher, my mind slipped back to a time when Frank and I were in the eighth grade. It was early morning before school began, and Frank and I were sitting in the classroom talking about the future. "What do you want to be when you grow up?" I asked him.

"A mortician," he replied.

"A mortician? Why would you want to do that?" I asked in dismay with my nose all scrunched up.

I will never forget the look of hurt in his eyes because he knew I did not understand his dream. "I was called to become a mortician, like one is called to the ministry," he patiently explained. Now God was going to allow him to minister to the people of his home town – a dream he had always had.

If we had very little money for pews and rolling stock, we had even less for advertising. We were not to worry. God knew that word of mouth was the best form of advertising and so, miraculously, the first eleven calls came from the eleven different communities in the county. Only God could have orchestrated that. We had provided caring, compassionate service, and God had made it possible for that word to quickly spread to each community.

We also wanted a way for folks to hear the daily obituaries. We asked the radio station for airtime, but we were turned down. Once again God provided. The very next week Frank attended a funeral directors' convention where he saw a product being sold that fit our needs perfectly. It was a phone line that anyone could call twenty-four hours a day, seven days a week and hear the latest obituaries. However, this program could only be sold to one business per town and we were that business. Another opportunity had been given to us by a loving and caring God.

In honor of God who had so graciously provided for us, we announced not only our obituaries but those of the other funeral home in town as well.

"Commit to the Lord whatever you do,
and your plans will succeed."

Proverbs 16:3 NIV

Did we have to make sacrifices when we followed God's call and went to Sylva? The answer was, "Yes." Basically, we reverted to the life we had known just after we were married and both of us were in school. At that time we struggled to pay the rent on our apartment, gas for the car, and our tuition. Because there were only so many places that we could cut expenses, we bought no clothes, spent no money on entertainment, never ate out, and in fact, ate only one meal a day. For dinner we would cook meals like spaghetti, foods that were inexpensive and filling. Because of all the practice we had gotten when we were in college, we had no problem slipping back into that life style again. The one place that we did not cut back was in our tithing. Each week we gave God his portion first. How could we have expected God to give us what we needed, if we were not willing to give the small amount that he asks us to give? Everything we have belongs to him anyway. He just allows us the privilege of using it and enjoying it while we are here. God also promises to supply all our needs if we will seek him and put him first in our hearts. Therefore, giving God ten percent should be our first thought.

Did God bless us beyond measure for our sacrifice? He certainly did! We had hoped to be able to pay off our debt in fifteen years, but we paid it off in seven! I find that fascinating since seven is the perfect number. God had told us that we were to open a funeral home in Sylva. With three of us in college, our two children and me, we certainly didn't have the needed capital to open such a business. But we obeyed God and trusted him to meet our every need, and he did. It was exciting just to wake up each morning with anticipation, eager to watch God at work in our lives — eager to see the miracles and blessings he would rain down upon us!

Frank in front of the new funeral home

God Had Other Plans for Me

Sometimes God tells us to do something that we would rather not. Perhaps we are afraid of failing, embarrassed at looking foolish, or simply do not want to be inconvenienced.

My good friend, Tina, had a memorable experience concerning a time when God spoke to her and told her to do something she really did not want to do. Unlike the time God told me to detour through Bethel and I disobeyed only to have my car totaled, Tina obeyed. Listen as she tells the story in her own words. It is a beautiful testament to what God can do through us for others if we will only obey.

> It had been a very busy morning! Getting my two children off to school and my husband and I off to work had been hectic – so hectic that I had not had time to prepare a salad that I needed to take to my Bible study luncheon that day.

> "It's okay," I thought. "I'll run by the grocery store when I leave work at noon, pick up what I need, run home, prepare the salad, and still make it to the luncheon by 1:00."

> I entered the grocery store and started down

the aisle when I passed a neighbor, to whom I smiled and spoke, and hurried on my way. When I got to the next aisle, God said, "Ask her to your home."

"Ask her to my home?" I thought, "I can't do that now, God, or I'll be late for my luncheon!"

"Ask her to your home," God said to me again, plain as day!

I stood there a moment more than a bit flustered and then, with quiet resolution, I retraced my steps until I once again stood near my neighbor.

"Would you like to come by my house?" I asked, secretly hoping that she would say, "No."

"Why yes, I would," she replied. "Thank you so much for the invitation."

As I drove home from the store I prayed, "God, I have no idea what all this is about. I have no idea what I am supposed to do or say, so please help me to know what to say and when to say it. Please lead, guide, and direct me as I visit with this woman."

It wasn't long before my neighbor walked through the door. I didn't have to wonder but a moment what this was all about because she immediately began to cry. Sitting on the couch, she poured out her heart to me. She was having an affair she explained, and she just needed to talk to someone. "I'm so thankful that you asked me here today," she cried, "because I know you are a guidance counselor, and I feel that you can help me."

Seated on the sofa, we talked for more than two hours while the salad fixings sat forgotten on the kitchen counter. At the end of that time, my neighbor came to realize that her family was too important to lose over another man, and she agreed to end her relationship with him.

As my neighbor left and I put away my unused groceries, I was reminded of the story in the eighth chapter of Acts when an angel of the Lord instructed Philip to go to the desert road. Philip obeyed, and on his way he met an important Ethiopian official to the queen. Because of this meeting, Philip was able to tell him the good news about Jesus, and the man believed and was baptized.

The Ethiopian in the Bible was saved and so was my neighbor's family. Since that day, I have made a concerted effort to slow down and become better at being aware of those around me. I try to watch for those near me who might be in need.

I have become better at seeing the hurt on faces around me. I try to watch for signs of loneliness or despair. I try to give hugs or ask the right questions. I try to make sure each person knows that I care and that I am ready and willing to help in any way I can.

And most of all, I pray as I go about my day that God will help me to slow down, to listen, and then to do what he wants me to do.

As I listened to Tina tell her story, I was reminded of a time when the Lord spoke to my Sunday school teacher, Pat McMillan, and told her to write a check for $200.00 and take it to the church. "But God," she replied, "I have my tithe offering check already written for this week!"

Again, God told her to write a check for $200.00 and take to the church, and again she asked God if he was sure that was what she was to do.

All morning she worked doing laundry and cleaning, and all day God hounded her about the $200.00. Finally, when God had not stopped insisting, she wrote another check and took both to the church.

On Sunday morning when she opened the church bulletin, the figures told her why God had insisted that she obey. Had she not written the check, the church would not have met their budget for the month. If we will just listen and obey, God will use us in big and small ways to make a difference.

Move Out of the Shallow End

Someone once wrote, "Great works are done in deep waters. If you're diving for pearls, you have to move out of the shallow end. Many of us never learn that lesson; fear restricts us to the comfort zone where we miss out on untold adventures and great peace. But Jesus tells us to launch out into the deep – in risk taking, in the pursuit of excellence, and in the knowledge of Him. We walk to the edge of all our light and that next step into the blackness holds the destiny God has for us. But it also holds whatever dangers lie in the darkness. We know that – we realize the risks, and because of that, perhaps we'll never take that one terrifying step that makes the miracles possible. No one ever said it would be easy out in the deep waters. No one ever guaranteed fair weather and smooth sailing. It's your choice – stay along the shore and you'll always be safe, but you'll also never know the blessings of the deep things of God." I would love to know who wrote that. I found it among my aunt's things after she died. It is so beautiful and so true.

When we had gone to Sylva and opened the funeral home, we had followed God into deep water and had experienced the joy of his love. When the Stovall's had waited as God had told them to do, they, too, had ventured into deep waters, and the result was health and healing for their son.

I encourage each of you to step out in faith and experience the blessings that await you in the knowledge of God.

Wait on the Lord

Earning my doctorate degree had always been a dream of mine; however, with two children in college, I knew I would have to wait to earn my PhD. Then an educational organization to which I belonged granted me a scholarship that paid one hundred percent of my graduate studies. In a few years, I was awarded my doctorate degree.

After graduation I began sending out applications for jobs that would allow me to use all I had learned while earning that degree. Because I knew that God had allowed me to fulfill my dream, I told him that I would go wherever he sent me and use what I had learned in my doctoral program for his glory.

As the days went by, I had gotten no job offers – not even the opportunity to interview. Now that we had moved to Sylva to open the funeral home, we felt that it was important for me to work in the same county – to be an integral part of the community. I had sent Jackson County an application when I sent out all the others but had heard nothing from them. "Well," I thought, "I have told God that I will go wherever he sends me; I will just need to wait for him to act. I'm sure he has something for me in mind."

A week later the phone rang about four o'clock one afternoon. It was my cousin, Frank Crawford, calling to tell me about an ad he had seen in the local newspaper. "Ann," he said in a voice filled with excitement, "this job sounds just like what you're looking for. It's for a curriculum specialist. Wasn't that part of your degree?"

"It was indeed. Is there a number to call?"

"Yes, it says to call 586-2311."

"I'll do it right now! Thank you so much for calling!"

I immediately dialed the number he had given me. My call was transferred to the Office of Assistant Superintendent who told me that the deadline for applying for the position ended at five o'clock that very afternoon. "Could I possibly come now and fill out an application?" I asked.

"You certainly may." Within minutes I was on my way to Sylva.

After talking with the assistant superintendent, I was told that I needed to return on Tuesday and interview for the job, which I did. I left work in Haywood County, drove to Sylva for the interview, and drove back to the school I had been working in that day. I told the principal what I had done, and he asked, "Have you told the superintendent here in Haywood County that you were interviewing?"

"No," I replied. "Do you think I should?"

"Most definitely."

I immediately picked up the phone and made the call. When I told the superintendent that I had interviewed for a job in another county, he said, "I know. They just called from Jackson County, and they want you to report to work at Blue Ridge School by seven thirty in the morning."

I had offered to go where ever God sent me, and God had taken me up on that offer. He had sent me to a K-12 school in a remote area of our state where I was to serve as the curriculum coordinator/assistant principal.

When I Open My Mouth, Let It Be Your Words That Come Out

*I*t was a fifty-minute drive to Blue Ridge School, and I spent all fifty minutes in prayer. I prayed for wisdom and guidance. I prayed that God would tell me what to do, when to do it, and how to do it, and that when I opened by mouth, it would be his words that came out. The entire fifty minutes of prayer was devoted to my new job. Throughout my prayers I claimed God's promise found in Mark 11:24 NRSV, "So I tell you, whatever you ask for in prayer, believe that you have received it, and it will be yours."

Blue Ridge School, I would discover later, had the lowest test scores in the county and in some areas, the lowest in the state. It was a school in crisis. But I did not know all this when I was told to report to work at 7:30 the next morning. Upon arriving at the school, I was given a tour of the building and then, along with the other staff members, went into a classroom where the principal was holding the first staff meeting of the school year.

At eight o'clock the meeting began with the principal welcoming everyone back and introducing the nine new faculty members. He introduced me last and before I sat down he said,

"Ann is our new curriculum coordinator, and whatever she says goes. If you are not happy with the decisions, you can go down the mountain. Now, there are donuts and coffee in the commons area. We will take about a fifteen minute break, and when we come back, I'll turn the meeting over to Ann."

I was in shock. What a way to begin a new job: having your boss turn everyone against you in the first thirty seconds! Needless to say, I did not go out for donuts and coffee! I stayed behind and prayed some more! I knew nothing – absolutely nothing – about the school, the school population, or the community. I did not know the school's strengths or its weaknesses. What was I supposed to talk about? Again I prayed, this time with even greater fervor, "Dear Heavenly Father, help me. When I open my mouth, please let it be your words that come out."

When everyone returned, I stood up and walked to the podium. We were in a high school classroom and everyone was sitting in desks which were arranged in straight rows facing the podium. The last thing I remember saying was, "Good morning." One and one-half hours later I came to. I woke up. I came to my senses. Call it what you like. But in that moment, I realized that all the desks were arranged in a circle and there was such a sense of family in that room! The teachers were sharing ideas, discussing issues, and planning for the opening of school. To this day, I do not know what was said or what went on during that hour and a half, but I know that God heard my prayer and when I opened my mouth it was his words that came out. In that hour and a half, a divided faculty came together and a spirit of "all for one and one for all" was born. Only God could have accomplished that! He had heard my prayers. He had answered.

In that morning a school was transformed. That morning I had trusted God, and he had not let me down. I had leaned not on my own understanding. That had certainly been easy enough as on that morning I had absolutely no understanding about the school, the students, the teachers, or the community. And I had no understanding about the strengths or weaknesses of any of those first three. What I did understand was the absolute power of God. I acknowledged him, and he directed our paths. He got us off to a wonderful start. He forged us into a team that was so strong there was nothing, with God's help, that could keep us from being successful.

In Ruth and Warren Myers book, *31 Days of Prayer*, is this wonderful prayer: "Thank you, Lord Jesus, that as a 'Christ-follower' I am called by Your noble and wonderful name. By Your undeserved favor, I have been made a member of Your royal family. Now I can approach You boldly, in Your merits alone. I expect You to answer my prayer because I came in Your name, concerned about what You want. What a privileged beggar I am!"

That morning so long ago God heard my pleading prayer and answered. I was and still am, and always will be, a privileged beggar before my God.

Just Thirty Minutes a Day

After my first day at Blue Ridge School, it became clear to me that I needed the help of my Heavenly Father who certainly knew the school's every need. I also knew that he was just waiting for me to ask for his help so that he could pour out his richest blessings. I believed that for this to happen I needed to walk more closely with the Lord. I needed more than my usual prayer time before going to sleep at night or the time I spent each evening after dinner reading the Bible. I needed a time when everything was so quiet that I truly felt that the only two awake were God and me – a time when I could listen better and hear him more clearly.

I thought of the many times I had read in the Bible when Jesus would arise early in the morning to talk with his Heavenly Father. It made perfect sense to me to go to the Lord early when you are rested, instead of at the end of the day when you are tired and stressed. Why not begin my day with my all-powerful, all-knowing God?

I had to get up at five-thirty in order to get to work by seven-thirty. Now I would just start getting up at five and spend that extra thirty minutes reading, praying, and listening. So, the next morning, and every morning thereafter, I got up at five o'clock and spent the first ten minutes reading the Bible, the second ten minutes praying, and the last ten minutes listening. I used *The One Year Bible*, which gives the reader a little of the Old Testament, a little of the New Testament, a Psalm and a Proverb every day. Reading a selection each day for 365 days, a person can read the entire Bible in a year.

It was amazing to me how the scripture for that particular day seemed to fit my situation, address my problem, or answer my question. I always made notes in the margin of my Bible and dated them. When I returned to that text in the coming years, I could then remember how God had met my needs on that day with that particular verse.

During my ten minutes of prayer, I prayed about my deepest concerns or questions for that day. I then spent the next ten minutes listening for God to tell me what I was supposed to do. Most of his answers came to me as ideas or as just a knowing – a certainty of how or what I was supposed to do.

The thirty minutes I spent each morning with the Lord became the most important thirty minutes of my every day. I soon learned that specific prayer requests brought specific answers. I could see that if one depended totally on God, life just got better and better.

I know that all the other thirty minutes I have spent with the Lord every morning since then have changed my life. It is a time when I am filled with peace after praying about a problem or relating a plan to God. The ten minutes of listening is a time of complete quiet, a time when I am filled with a calmness and peace that sustain me throughout a very hectic day. Sometimes it is a time of healing for my soul – a healing of the hurt and heartache that can come as a part of day to day living.

I encourage you to seek the presence of God. Find a time and place where you can draw near to God, and he will draw near to you. Andrew Murray wrote, "The nearness of God gives us rest and power in prayer. This nearness is given to the person who makes God's intimate presence a priority. Seek nearness to God, and He will give it. God's nearness makes it easy to pray in faith. So persevere. Learn to place yourself in His presence, to quietly anticipate His drawing near, and then to begin to pray."

Ruth Warren, using scripture verses, wrote a wonderful prayer to pray during our quiet times in God's presence: "Dear Father, how I long to know You better. Reveal Yourself to me in new ways as I wait quietly before You. Make Yourself more real to me than anyone or anything on earth. Open my eyes to see You in the Scriptures; quiet my mind and emotions to be still and know that You are God. Calm my heart, taking away my strain and stress. Make me conscious of Your presence as I wait before You with holy reverence."

Taking God into the Workplace

During my first two weeks as curriculum specialist at Blue Ridge School, I did a needs assessment. The results were all too clear. The school had serious problems that would require divine help. While I was praying every morning for the school, I wanted others at the school to do the same. I wanted them to see the results of making God a partner in our improvement efforts. I wanted them to experience the power of two or more gathering together to talk with the Lord. I began by asking four teachers if they would be willing to take about ten minutes every morning and meet me for prayer. I truly believed the scripture when it said that where two or more are gathered, there Jesus is also.

The five of us agreed to meet each morning in the computer lab and to come with a list of problems or concerns that needed prayer – a list we would have written down on a slip of paper before entering the room. Our plan was to read over the five lists and to spend the next ten minutes in silent prayer. We prayed for students or parents who were having problems, for issues or concerns within the school, or even for problems within the community that impacted the school. Not only did we claim the promise God made in Matthew 7:7-8 NIV, ("Ask and it will be given to you; seek and you will find; knock and the door will be opened to you. For everyone who asks receives; he who seeks finds; and to him who knocks, the door will be opened."), but we also claimed the promise that he made in 2 Corinthians 9:8 KJV when he said that he is at work in all things. It was amazing to see God at work as he seemed to be checking off our list of problems one by one. Remember, only God can give true significance to your work or activities. Call on him to prosper all that you do.

Daily, with God as our teacher, we became a family. God took individuals from diverse backgrounds and experiences and molded us into a body that was willing to help one another do what was best for the school. The high school teachers took part of their planning time to help the elementary teachers with such things as science experiments, and the elementary teachers agreed to tutor older students who were having problems. Little by little and day by day, God was improving our school.

Daily we prayed that God would send us teachers who truly wanted to be in our unique setting. Not only did God hear our prayers and answer, but he sent us very special and extraordinary individuals. It wasn't long before the school was filled with teachers who were not only brilliant in their field of study but who loved their profession and loved children. God sent us teachers who had a passion for the Lord and compassion for young people. Those teachers who chose to stay at the school and the new ones that came formed a powerful bond that resonated throughout everything we did.

At the end of that first year, Blue Ridge School's end-of-grade-test scores rose from last place in the county to second place! God had blessed us indeed!

I encourage you to commit all that you do to the Lord. Ask him to work in and through you. Pray specifically about the things you are doing. God is the only one who can give real significance to your work.

They Are So Bright But ...

*G*od sent so many wonderful teachers to Blue Ridge School, but there is one that sticks out clearly in my mind. This young man exemplified the power of God to act on our behalf. I also think that the way he came to us was extraordinary.

Rick Plotts worked in an automobile plant in Detroit and was in our area on vacation with his wife and young child. He loved the area. He enjoyed hiking. He loved the mountains and the lakes. He very much wanted to stay in the area, but, of course, to do that he would need a job. Rick spoke five languages fluently and had always wanted to teach, but he did not have his teaching certification. We desperately needed a Spanish teacher. With the help of the central office, we hired him and helped him earn his teaching certificate. Rick truly walked with God, and his presence and influence impacted the school in a most positive way. He was, however, working with students who lived in a very remote area and who saw no need to ever learn a foreign language.

Rick had been praying daily for his Spanish classes as had we, the prayer team. However, one Friday a couple weeks before spring break, he walked into my office, sat down, put his head in his hands, and said, "I don't know what else to do. These students are so bright, but they don't do their homework, they don't participate in class, they just do not seem to care about learning Spanish."

"Well, Rick," I said, "if you lived in these coves and valleys and never saw yourself leaving the area, would you feel the need to learn Spanish? We need to give them a reason to learn the language. We need to immerse them in the language and culture of a Spanish speaking country. How about if we take them to the Yucatan Peninsula over spring break? Do you think you can plan such a trip for your thirteen students and the two of us and tell me by Monday how much it will cost per person?"

"I can," he replied, "but where would we get the money for such a trip?"

"You make the plans. I'll find the money."

When Rick left my office, I began to pray, counting on God to provide. That evening I attended a dinner at a local country club where I was introduced to a young man who was quite well-to-do and who happened to ask about our school. God had provided the opportunity for me to share our need with him. When I left the club, I had the promise of enough money for two students to go to Mexico no matter what the cost.

On Monday Rick reported that we could spend the week of spring break in the Yucatan and visit all the historic sites for three hundred forty-nine dollars per person. "Let's do it!" I said. "You talk to the parents and work out all the details, and I'll get the money."

That evening I called Bob Ingle who owned a chain of grocery stores in our area. I explained who I was and told him I had called to make him a proposition. I would stock the shelves in his grocery store near the school, mop the floors, and clean the toilets, whatever it took to earn three hundred and forty-nine dollars. When he asked why I needed the money, I explained our problem and our solution. We planned to immerse our students into the culture and language of Mexico and thus create within them the desire to learn Spanish.

The next day the school secretary walked into my office with a check for seven hundred dollars, enough to pay the way of two of our students. With a few more phone calls to local businesses with the same offer, to do whatever I needed in order to earn three hundred forty-nine dollars, we had enough money to pay the way for all thirteen students. The fifteen of us were on our way to Mexico!

When we stepped off the plane, we told the students, "You have had eight months of Spanish and the opportunity to learn the basic conversational skills you will need to function during the next week. Therefore, do not ask us how to locate a restroom or how to order something to eat. You are on your own in that regard."

That first day we toured the ruins of Uxmal and afterwards went to a nearby hotel so that the students could swim and have dinner before we returned to the ruins for the evening light show. We were the only ones in the pool and hadn't been there more than ten minutes when in walked a young man Rick's age with thirteen young Mexicans. Immediately Rick went to him and introduced himself. He explained that he taught Spanish in the states. It turned out that the young man was an English teacher in Mexico. "My students are very bright," he said, "but they just don't seem interested in learning English."

For the next week, those two teachers and twenty-six students spent a great deal of time together. When we left Mexico a week later, our students were much more fluent in Spanish, and I'm sure the Mexican students were more proficient in English. Only God could have orchestrated that!

The next year the number of students who registered for

Spanish tripled, and the year after that we were forced to add Spanish III to the list of courses offered. The travel opportunities also expanded. The Spanish I students continued to travel to the Yucatan Peninsula, and the Spanish II students always went to Mexico City.

We had depended on God to help us, and he had met our every need. It is truly an amazing thing to watch God at work!

He Set Us on High

When I went to Blue Ridge School, the middle school and high school students shared the same part of the building and had the same teachers. Such a situation definitely was not the best situation for the middle school students. They needed their own area and teachers who were committed to their age group. We began by selecting teachers who loved working with middle school students, and we brought in mobile units to develop a middle school on another part of the campus.

As we worked to develop a middle school program, we knew that we wanted to develop not only the mind but the character of each student. We wanted our students to leave middle school believing in themselves – believing that there was nothing they could not do if they worked hard enough. We wanted the students to develop inner strength and inner beauty and to see this same strength and beauty in others.

To develop these skills, we went outside the walls of the traditional classroom and into nature. The students would need to see that it is neither clothes nor popularity that is really important in the larger scheme of life, but it is what's inside a person. We designed a program that built upon the previous year and got progressively more challenging.

In the sixth grade the students participated in a teambuilding program that not only taught the importance of teamwork but also sought to improve thinking and reasoning skills. The second part of this program occurred in the seventh grade. The students were put through a low ropes course, and in the eighth grade, those same students were put through a challenging high ropes course. It was interesting to see the most self-centered girls and boys fall apart on some of the more difficult parts of the course and have to depend on the students they had teased and tormented in the past to talk them through the rough spots and help them succeed. These students that had been so unkind to others in the past began to see the inner strength and beauty of those they had not previously appreciated, and all the students began to look deeper than clothes or outward appearances when determining a person's true worth. And all the middle school students began to understand the value of team work.

In the sixth grade, the students were taken on a camping trip and an extensive and difficult hike. They were taught survival skills such as how to read a compass, build a shelter, and find food and water. In the seventh grade, this same project became more difficult as rock climbing was added, and the lessons of survival became more intense. In the eighth grade, the students participated not only in rock climbing but in repelling, too. Many learned that they could accomplish things they never thought they had the courage to even try. And as before, it was the students that some had looked down on in the past who excelled, and some who had been so "cool" suddenly did not appear to be worthy of that accolade.

In the sixth grade, the students were taken white water rafting. It seemed that "mister cool dude" was always the one to fall into the river and think he was going to drown, and it was always the little chubby guy Mr. Cool had constantly teased who came to his rescue. In the seventh grade, spelunking was added to the program, and in the eighth grade, the students spent the night in the cave two levels down. Because taking care of the earth was a big part of this program, the students took turns carrying the "honey pots" into the cave and out. Carrying a honey pot out of a cave after a long night can be a sobering and most humbling experience.

And so the program went, with activities that taught the students to look deep within themselves and find that inner strength and determination needed to get a job done. They learned the value of hard work and listening. They learned the value of teamwork and the importance of looking deeper than clothes or outward appearance when selecting a team member. They learned all this and much more. These lessons carried over into the classroom and day by day their studies in math, science, language arts, etc. took on new meaning and greater importance. When these students left middle school, they were better prepared to meet the rigors of high school as well as the outside world. They had learned decision-making skills as well as survival skills, and they were ready to become all that they could be.

At the end of the first year, this team of middle school teachers was named Middle School Team of the Year by Western Carolina University.

God was with us in the planning of this program, and he was certainly there as we carried it out. No student was ever injured. No parent was ever upset with us. Only God could have accomplished that.

Our dependence on the Lord for direction, along with our team efforts and hard work, brought us amazing results! God truly delivered us and set us on high. At the end of the first year, we had the second highest test scores in the county. When the test results were announced, I panicked! I was afraid that the central office would think that we had cheated — that we had somehow found a way to beat the system. Amazingly, not one negative word was said. At the end of the second year, our test scores were ranked first in the county, and the honors poured in. The governor of our state named us an Entrepreneurial School and brought the entire faculty to the capitol for a banquet. God had indeed exalted us.

But that was not surprising to me. I believe God is always there, waiting patiently to hear from us. He eagerly wishes to rain down his richest blessing upon us. He waits for us to ask, to obey, to trust, to look to him, to set our love upon him, and to know his name so that he can deliver us, and set us on high.

Not Just a Pump Knot

One of our most important jobs here on earth is to pray for others – intercessory prayer. I do not think that our son would be with us today if thousands of people had not been praying for him throughout his ordeal.

In Hebrews 7:25 KJV we are told that Jesus lives to make intercession for us. As an example of the importance and power of intercessory prayer, one needs only to think of what Christ does following his crucifixion – he now sits at the right hand of God and makes intercession for us. Are we not called to become like Christ? Is it not our chief goal in life to become more Christlike? If that be the case, then intercessory prayer must be one of our main jobs.

Intercessory prayer is extremely powerful! Once you get into the habit of praying for those around you throughout the day, God will not only hear and answer your prayers, he will provide you with "a knowing". By this I mean that the Holy Spirit will speak to you and tell you what you need to know in order to help that person. You will become one with Him in spirit. An example of this occurred one day as I was leaving work. As I was walking out of the building I passed a teacher assistant and a small boy sitting on a bench in the hallway. I overheard the teacher assistant say, "I have called your mom, and she is on her way. Now don't cry because you're going to be just fine."

I walked over to the pair and asked, "What's wrong?"

"Oh, he just fell and got a big pump knot on his head."

"Let me see," I said and the child pulled an ice pack away from his forehead to expose a large knot.

Before I could say anything, Patty, the teacher assistant, said, "I've told him that he is going to be just fine. I have a knot much bigger than his on my head that I have had for a long time, and I am fine."

"You have a knot on your head, and it's been there a long time?" I asked Patty.

"I sure do," she replied.

"Will you show me?" I asked.

"Sure, it's right here," she said, as she pulled back her hair. Reaching for my hand she said, "You can feel how big it is."

The moment I touched that knot I knew it was something bad – I knew it was cancer. "How long has the knot been there?" I asked.

"Two years or more."

"Have you ever seen a doctor about it?"

"Yes, one time a year or so ago when I had taken one of my girls to the pediatrician, I showed it to him, and he said it was probably nothing to worry about."

"Patty, I want you to promise me that when you leave here today you will go to another doctor and get a second opinion. Promise me that you will not go home until you have done that. I don't want to scare you, but that could be very serious. It could be malignant."

The child's mother picked him up, Patty promised to see a doctor, and I began my drive home. The next day at school, I was told that Patty had been sent immediately to Duke University Hospital for tests. Days went by without any word, and then one day we heard that Patty had a rare form of cancer. It was so rare that there were only three other cases in the United States.

When she finally returned to work, she came into my office and closed the door. "I don't know what I am going to do," she cried. "I'm worried about what will become of my two girls."

Putting my arm around her, I said, "Patty, you are probably not going to believe me and my words may not relieve one moment of your anxiety, but you are going to be fine." As I had silently prayed, God had told me this. And today Patty *is* just fine!

Because I believe so completely in the power of intercessory prayer, every time I pass an ambulance with lights and siren blaring, I pray for the person that ambulance is rushing to help or for the individual inside. I pray for wisdom and discernment for the doctors that will be treating that person. When I pass a person on the street who appears sad or upset or down on their luck, I pray for them.

Daily we come in contact with people who need our prayers, and because I know that God hears and answers, we must pray. It costs us nothing. It requires little, if any, extra time, but it pays big dividends.

One has only to read Joshua 10:12-14 LB to see the power of intercessory prayer in action. The Bible tells us that as the men of Israel were pursuing their foe, Joshua prayed aloud, "Let the sun stand still over Gibeon, and let the moon stand in its place over the valley of Aijalon!" And we are told the sun and the moon didn't move until the Israeli army had finished the destruction of its enemies – all because of the prayer of one man!

A Lesson Not Learned Until Later

$\mathcal{M}$y driving time has always been part of my prayer time. One day in 1993 as I was driving home from work at Blue Ridge School, my prayers were all for Annas Jones. I really didn't know Annas well, but I liked him. Annas was one of the three men who worked in the maintenance department for the school system. He was such a shy man who always hung back and allowed his co-workers to take center stage. The other two men were always cutting up and carrying on — full of fun and energy — but Annas usually remained quiet. However, he always had a smile. Now Annas was dying. His illness had begun suddenly and progressed rapidly until now his vital organs were shutting down. The family had been called in.

I prayed that God would put his healing hands on Annas and allow his healing, strengthening powers to flow into him and miraculously heal him. As I prayed, God spoke to me. His message was clear and simple, "Go lay hands on Annas and pray."

My response was immediate. "I don't think I can do that. I've never laid hands on anyone and prayed. I just don't feel comfortable doing that. And you know, God, that I do not feel comfortable praying aloud. I just would not feel comfortable praying in front of Annas' family. Besides, God, they will only allow the immediate family into ICU. They are not going to let me in." All the way home my excuses continued, and all the way home God continued to insist that I go lay hands on Annas and pray. When I arrived home, I quickly changed my clothes and began working in the yard. I thought if I worked hard enough I would not be able to hear God. By night fall, there was not a weed left in the yard. Not only had I pulled weeds, but I had raked, trimmed the shrubs, and gathered limbs and brush into a pile. The yard was perfect. I was exhausted, but still God's insistence continued. I went inside and began to clean. By eight thirty I had washed, dusted, vacuumed, and cleaned until there was little left to be done, and still God's insistence continued. I think this episode illustrates the patience of God. Remember when God told Jonah to go to Nineveh, and Jonah refused. God caused him to be swallowed by a whale. Instead, God called to me in another way.

Suddenly the phone rang. It was Annas's wife, Peggy, trying to get in touch with my cousin who lived above me. It was as if God himself had phoned me. After telling her where she could locate my cousin, I said, "Peggy, you don't really know me, and when I tell you what I am about to tell you, you are probably going to think I'm crazy. Today, as I was driving home from work, God told me that I was to go to Annas, lay hands on him, and pray."

Peggy's response was immediate. "I'll pick you up at eight-thirty in the morning." God had just granted me admittance into ICU.

The next morning Peggy picked me up, and by nine thirty we were in the ICU. "Now, I sense that you are uncomfortable with this, so I will pray first," Peggy said.

I wanted to say, "Lady, you have no idea how uncomfortable I am!"

Peggy prayed aloud, and when she stopped, I laid my hands on Annas and began quietly praying. At that time in my life, praying aloud was very difficult for me. Therefore, I prayed silently. When I had finished, I said, "Amen," and we left. When we got to the car, I said to Peggy, "God told me that your husband's recovery is going to be long and drawn out, but he *will* be fine." And that is exactly what happened. His recovery took many months, but in the end he was fine. He never returned to work. Instead he retired and turned his basement into a wonderful workshop where he made clocks and many other beautiful wooden objects.

After this experience I wondered if I had been given the gift of healing. I waited, thinking God would ask me to do something like this again. He didn't. I didn't understand. It would be three years before I would come to understand why God had told me to go to Annas.

*When my daughter-in-law, Carla, picks up a new book to read, she turns to the last chapter immediately and reads it first to learn how the story ends. If you just can't wait to know why God sent me to Annas, you may turn to the chapter titled "A Lesson Learned" and read it next.

*Annas Jones holding one of the many beautiful
clocks he made in his shop after his recovery*

The Prayer of the Opened or Closed Door

While I was working at Blue Ridge School, the director of the Exceptional Children's Program was slated to retire, and the position would soon become available. I was asked by central office and encouraged by all the school principals to take the position. While it was not a position I really wanted, their encouragement was difficult to ignore. Finally, I agreed to apply for the job while asking God to take complete control of the whole situation. "Please, God," I prayed, "if this is not your will for my life, please just close the door that has been opened. Please do not allow me to make a mistake by taking a job that is not best or right for me. Only you know what the future holds. Please keep me on your pathway for my life."

A couple of weeks later I was told that I had gotten the job. The superintendent asked me to attend the board meeting where I would be introduced. My introduction was the last item on the agenda. At ten o'clock when it was time for my introduction, the chairman of the board turned to her right and said something quietly to a board member. Then she said aloud, "This appointment is not going to fly."

The meeting was adjourned and everyone just sat there trying to figure out what had happened. Finally, folks slowly made their way out of the building and to their cars.

The next morning, not sure what had happened, I reported to the central office and went straight to the superintendent's office. He and I had been friends for a long time, and so we could speak freely with one another.

"Ann," he began, "I don't know what happened. I just know that you did not get the job."

I sat there for a moment, saying nothing, and then got up to leave. "Aren't you angry?" he asked.

"No," I said. "Why would I be angry?"

"Well, the chairman of the board has just kept you from getting the job!"

"Really?" I replied. "You and I have known one another for a long time. We are both Christians. Are you telling me that you think the chairman of the school board is more powerful than God? If I was supposed to have that job, then I would have it. When I agreed to apply for that position, I told God what I was going to do, and I asked him to take complete control of everything. Obviously, he did not want me in that position, or I would be there."

"So what are you going to do now?" he asked.

"I'm going back to Blue Ridge where it is clear God intends for me to be."

I had trusted God to close that door if it was not one I should have walked through. Now I just needed to wait patiently for God to show me what to do next.

I have a very dear friend, Anne Culpepper, whose husband

was killed in an automobile accident when their three daughters were eight, thirteen, and fifteen. She did the most remarkable job of rearing those girls and was able to make difficult decisions and advise her daughters with confidence and peaceful assurance. When I asked her about this, she told me that she prays: "God, I have made my decision. If this decision is *not* part of your perfect plan, then please close the door – prevent this from happening. If it *is* part of your plan, God, then open the door – allow it to take place."

God Is in Control of My Life

$\mathcal{A}$ couple of months before the end of the school year the principal called me into his office and told me that he planned to retire. He asked if I planned to apply for his position. "I don't know," I said. "I will spend a couple of days out in the community talking to folks to determine the support I would have, and I will let you know."

A few days later, on a Friday, I did just that. I went first to the home of the school board member from that community. After I explained why I was there, he told me, "Ann, if you decide to apply for the job of principal, you will most certainly have my support. But I must tell you that I am hearing another name for this position coming from the central office."

I thanked him, and without going anywhere else, I returned to school. I immediately went to the principal's office and told him what I had been told. "I will not be applying for the position," I told him. "Central office has already made their decision."

Now I want to tell you that the enemy is always near and when you are troubled about things, he will try to discourage you. He will try to make you think that God doesn't have your best interests in mind. At these times you must ask God to strengthen your faith. You must go to him in prayer more often and search the scriptures more carefully.

In this situation, less than two hours after I talked to the principal and told him that I would not be applying for the job, the superintendent walked into my office. "Now, Ann, I understand that you are hearing rumors concerning a particular applicant. I want you to know that I have never talked to the person whose name you have heard. If you want the position of principal, you have my support."

At that I put up my hand to stop him, and I said, "It doesn't matter because you, as superintendent, will have no effect on my professional career. The chairman of the school board will have no effect on my professional career. I will be where I am supposed to be next year because God is in control of my life."

Without saying another word, he got up and walked out of my office, and I looked around to determine who had just spoken. "Surely," I thought, "that did not just come out of my mouth!"

I knew that I had to get away by myself and think. I went into the office and told the secretary that I needed to take the afternoon off. I left the school and drove down the mountain and into town. My church was having a huge flea market the next day, and folks were preparing for that. I had planned to go to the church after school and paint birdhouses to sell. Now, with extra time on my hands, I did just that. Since everyone was working in the church basement, I gathered all my materials and went to the third floor where I could be alone.

It wasn't long, however, before I heard a voice say, "Has anyone seen Ann Melton?" It was the chairman of the school board.

It hadn't taken her long to find me. "Now, Ann," she began, "I know what you are hearing."

I put my hand up to stop her, and again the same words escaped my lips. "It does not matter because you, as chairman of the board, will have no effect on my professional career. The superintendent will have no effect on my professional career. I will be where I am supposed to be next year because God is in control of my life." And for the second time that day, the person I had just spoken to got up and left the room without saying a word. And for the second time that day, I looked around hoping someone else had spoken those words. Surely I had not just said them! "Will I even have a job come Monday morning?" I wondered.

Strangely enough, the only thing that happened on Monday was that the principal brought me my mail and right on top was an advertisement for the position of elementary language arts consultant at the Western Regional Service Alliance (WRESA) serving the seventeen counties of western North Carolina. The moment I held the advertisement in my hand I knew that God intended for me to apply.

A few weeks later I interviewed for the position and got it! The words that had so prophetically come from my mouth had been true! I was going to be where God had intended for me to be! I had declared to those in authority that God would rescue me. I had trusted God to place me where he wanted me, and he had blessed me for that.

"Oh, how great is your goodness to those who publicly declare that you will rescue them. For you have stored up great blessings for those who trust and reverence you."

Psalm 31:19 LB

Just a Stepping Stone

*I*loved the job at WRESA. I truly felt that I was using my doctorate to serve many other people, students, teachers, and staff alike. It was a job that required long hours and much driving, but I was happy. I loved meeting new people, and I met new ones every day. One day the new superintendent of Madison County came into my office. She needed materials and information on various reading programs. We talked for a long time, and it was as if I had known her all my life. When she got up to leave, she turned and asked, "Would you be willing to come to Madison County as Assistant Superintendent in charge of curriculum and instruction?"

"I will certainly think about it," I told her "and I'll give you a call."

Over the next two weeks, I prayed about the decision, and I felt God leading me to take the job. However, when the director of WRESA heard that I had been offered the job and that I was seriously considering it, he came to my office to try and talk me out of going. "You can't go to Madison County," he said. "They hire and fire over there at the drop of a hat. You won't last six months!"

"I appreciate your concern," I said. "I really do. But I have prayed about this, and I feel that God opened this door and that he expects me to walk through it. I feel that he sent me to Blue Ridge School, and I know that he accomplished wonderful things there. I believe that he has great plans for me in Madison County also. I believe he put me here at WRESA to get me to Madison County. I'm sorry, but I think this was just a stepping stone in God's plan for me." With that remark, I once again put myself in God's hands and stepped back, waiting eagerly and prayerfully to see just what he would accomplish next.

God Will Counsel You with His Eye on You

"I will instruct you and teach you the way you should go; I will counsel you with my eye upon you."
Psalm 32:8 NRSV

Once again, I was going somewhere that I knew nothing, absolutely nothing, about. I knew nothing about Madison County, the schools within the county, the students, the teachers, or the administrators. I was walking into the job depending totally on God and his promises. In Psalm 119:26 LB it says, "I told you my plans and you replied. Now give me your instructions. Make me understand what you want; for then I shall see your miracles." Once again I would claim the promises of God and expect miracles!

The first thing I did upon arriving in the Madison County school system was to do a needs assessment just as I had done at Blue Ridge School. What I discovered was that the system was actually just a bigger Blue Ridge School, and I could apply all that I had learned there. Every program I had begun at Blue Ridge, I could now start in Madison County. All the materials I had used at Blue Ridge, I could use in Madison County. It was amazing!

God had put me through seven years of boot camp to prepare me for this! He had counseled me for seven years, and I knew he would continue to keep his eye on me. I knew I could step out in confidence, knowing he would lead, guide, and direct me if I continued to rely on him. And like Blue Ridge, the improvement was amazing! When I arrived in Madison County, the school system, based on its test scores, was ranked seventy-second out of one hundred in the state. At the end of the first year, it was ranked twenty-fourth. At the end of the second year, every school was named an Exemplary School; three were named Schools of Excellence, and two were named Schools of Distinction! I was reminded of a promise God made in the book of John that reads: "I am the vine, you are the branches. Those who abide in me and I in them bear much fruit, because apart from me you can do nothing" (John 15:5 NRSV).

We all hope and pray that our lives will make a difference to the people around us, to our loved ones, to our communities, and to the world. As Christians, we want to bear fruit for the Lord. Fortunately, God does not expect us to do this without help. He promises that if we will abide in him, if we will walk with him daily talking and listening, and if we spend time in his word, he will work through us so that our efforts bring fruitful results. I believe that the difference in bearing fruit and bearing much fruit is in the degree to which we pursue God – the degree to which we yield ourselves to him and his will. If we have the courage to dedicate our lives to God, to truly listen for his guidance, and to rely upon his strength, there is no limit to what we can accomplish in his name.

God Will Meet Our Needs

When I did the needs assessment for Madison County Schools, I realized that the teachers there lacked the basic tools that they needed to do their job. Each class did not have enough dictionaries for the children to use during writing activities. They did not have encyclopedias needed for research. Simple tools such as class sets of rulers or manipulatives were not available for math lessons. In order to get the money, the math coordinator and I wrote a grant that gave us eighty thousand dollars. Every penny of that money was used to purchase materials for the classrooms. Not only did we provide needed materials for the teachers, we also provided staff development programs that would show the teachers how to use the new materials.

Over the next three years, we wrote many other grants. Each grant took us hours upon hours to write. We did not have the luxury of only writing the grant; we had to continue doing our jobs while we wrote. And then, once the grant money was allotted, we spent many hours planning and presenting staff development classes for all the teachers and teacher assistants in the county. We did not simply provide hundreds of hours of staff development – we provided thousands of hours. During those years, I kept God's promise made in Isaiah 40:31 NIV clearly before me and he kept that promise – "…but those who hope in the Lord will renew their strength. They will soar on wings like eagles; they will run and not grow weary, they will walk and not be faint." In spite of the hours spent writing grants and the hours of sleep lost in the process, in spite of the hours spent preparing and presenting staff development on top of an already full daily schedule, in spite of all these demands which we imposed upon ourselves, I don't ever remember being exhausted. I don't ever know of a time that we felt so weary that we considered giving up. It seemed that the more we did the more energized we felt. I also knew that our strength came only from God.

The needs assessment showed that we needed a math program for grades K-5 that was hands on and interactive. I contacted high performing schools and talked with their principals to determine which math programs they were using. I then visited many of those schools to see the programs first hand and talk with the teachers that were using them. At the same time, Kathy Fefer, the math coordinator, was working just as hard to find the program we needed. After several weeks, the right program still had not been found. One afternoon Kathy walked into my office, slumped into a chair, and with a voice filled with frustration said, "I give up. The program that we are looking for is just not out there!"

"Well," I replied, "we have done everything within our power to find the program we need. Now we will just have to turn it over to the Lord and wait for him to provide it for us."

Three days later, my phone rang and a man said, "Hi, my name is David Bramlett, and I am a principal of a public school in Oklahoma. My teachers have developed a math program that we believe is very good. I am coming to your area soon, and I would appreciate the opportunity to show you our program."

We scheduled the meeting, and two weeks later Mr. Bramlett

arrived at our office. I was meeting with some parents. I asked Kathy if she would go ahead with the meeting, and I would join them as soon as I could. Thirty minutes later the door of my office opened, and there stood Kathy with a huge smile, giving me the two thumbs up signal. The new program was exactly what we were looking for. It was so popular with the students and teachers, that when I left the central office, I had enough grant money to order six more years of the program and store it for future use.

God had once again heard my prayers and had again met our needs. He had not only delivered a good math program, but he had delivered the right math program – the program that exactly met our needs! I had claimed the promise of 2 Chronicles 16:9 LB, which says that the Lord goes to and fro across the earth on our behalf. I could easily imagine him being present in those Oklahoma classrooms, watching those students at work and saying, "This is exactly what they need in Madison County!"

When I think of Blue Ridge School or Madison County Schools and my years there, I know that God richly blessed us because of our faith. We must, I believe, beware of limiting God, not only by our unbelief, but also by thinking that we know what he can do. We must always expect unexpected things! In Ephesians 3:20 LB it says, "Now glory be to God who by his mighty power at work within us is able to do far more than we would ever dare to ask or even dream of – infinitely beyond our highest prayers, desires, thought, or hopes." We must expect great things of our God!

A Lesson Learned

On Sunday, December 1, 1996, my husband suffered a massive heart attack. I had been to Sunday school and was walking into the sanctuary when suddenly I knew that I needed to go home instead of attending church. When I arrived home, I found my husband in the throes of a major heart attack. He was taken to the Haywood County Hospital emergency room. He died once on the way there, was revived, and died again in the emergency room. Again he was revived.

Later that night, after family and friends had left the hospital, our son, our daughter, and I had turned out the lights in the ICU waiting room and were trying to go to sleep when our son suddenly got up, turned on the light, and announced that we must pray. Standing in the center of that room with hands joined, he prayed the sweetest prayer I have ever heard. Then he walked over to the phone, called his pastor, and asked if the verse that speaks of laying on hands meant joining hands as we had done or if it specifically meant that we should lay our hands on Frank and pray. After debating the question for several minutes, our son hung up the phone and said, "We're not going to take any chances. We are going down to Dad's room, lay our hands on him, and pray – which we did.

The next morning Frank was transported to Mission Hospital, twenty-five miles away. His life hung in the balance. That night the waiting room was filled with friends and relatives. Suddenly, a man walked out of the crowd, came up to me, and said, "You don't know me, but God has sent me to tell you that your husband is going to be fine." He asked to pray with our children and me, and then he was gone.

Suddenly my mind raced back to the day God sent me to the bedside of Annas Jones. At that time I did not understand what I was to learn from that experience. Now, three years later, I understood that if God had not sent me to pray over Annas and then told me he would be fine, I would not have completely believed the messenger God had just sent to me. This realization filled me with such peace as I finally understood the lesson God had for me.

The Gift of Healing

*B*ecause my husband suffered his heart attack on December 1, I had never completed our Christmas shopping. Two weeks later while in a store buying Christmas gifts I happened to overhear a conversation between the shop owner and a customer. It seemed the customer's wife had been diagnosed with cancer and was not doing well. The shop owner suggested that the customer call a preacher by the name of Ron Childress who had the gift of healing. After the customer left, I went to the shop owner and said, "I'm sorry, but I couldn't help but overhear your conversation. My husband recently suffered a massive heart attack, and I wonder if you would be willing to give me Ron Childress's phone number?"

"Of course," he replied.

The next day at work things were quiet, and so I dialed the number I had been given. When Reverend Childress answered, I explained that I was calling about my husband who was very ill. He listened carefully, and after a long pause, he said, "We are going to pray for your husband, but first we're going to pray for you. I want you to place your right hand over your right eye. There is something seriously wrong behind that eye." I did what he told me. I placed my hand over my eye, and he prayed that my eye would be healed. Next he asked that I place my right hand over my abdomen because he said there was a problem there. Again I did as he told me, and again he prayed for my healing. Then he prayed for Frank's healing and told me that when I got home that evening I was to lay my hands on Frank and pray for him, and he would be fine.

Did I believe in the power of God to heal? Did I believe in the power of laying on hands and calling on the Lord to allow his healing strengthening power to flow through me and provide healing? The answer to both questions was an unequivocal, "Yes." I had seen it happen in my own life with one of my children.

When our oldest child was in the first grade, she came home from school one day with her ankles and legs swollen to twice their normal size. I immediately called our pediatrician but was told that he was out of town. I was referred to another doctor who, upon examining her, placed her in the hospital.

Two days later our regular doctor returned, but the two physicians did not agree on either a diagnosis or a treatment. In the end, we stayed with our doctor who felt that Myra had rheumatic fever and should be on penicillin and complete bed rest. She was not even allowed to walk to the bathroom. Each week we had to take her to the lab for blood work, and each week her condition grew worse. One day, after returning from the doctor's office where we had been told that her sedimentation rate was the highest it had ever been and the treatment did not seem to be working, there was a knock at the door. When I opened it, there stood two people, a man and a woman, deacons from our church. They came inside and visited with us briefly. When they got up to leave, they asked if they could pray for Myra. "Please do so," I urged.

Laying their hands on Myra, they prayed for her, and in that moment she was healed! When Frank came home from work that evening, he did what he always did the moment he walked through the door. He scooped Myra up in his arms and immediately placed his fingers on her wrist to take her pulse and to determine her sedimentation rate.

This time the look of shock on Frank's face really alarmed me! "What's her sed rate?" I asked, fearing the worst.

"It's normal!" he replied, his voice shaking.

"Normal?" I said. "Please take her pulse, and figure it again!" He took her pulse and refigured it. The second time the results were the same.

The next morning I called the doctor and made an appointment to take Myra in. She was sent to the lab for blood work and then to the doctor's office. After an anxious wait, we were ushered into the examining room. The doctor examined her, and then picking up the lab report he turned to me with tears in his eyes and announced, "Her sed rate is normal!"

This occurred just days before Christmas. It was a wonderful gift, when, on Christmas day, Myra could be up playing with her younger brother. She had gone from complete bed rest to being an active seven year old in a matter of days!

Myra and her brother visiting Santa
a few days before Christmas

Certainly I had faith in the power of God to heal. Most definitely I had believed in the healing power of laying on hands. Was Frank not still alive after his 1996 heart attack when the children and I laid hands on him and prayed? Was he not still alive when the doctors did not feel he would live through the night? Certainly, he was still with us because God is able to do mighty miracles! As children of God, we have a power at work within us that can do miraculous things! We have only to claim God's promises and believe that he will keep them.

So, as I spoke with Reverend Childress, I recalled these incidents and trusted in the power of God to heal both my husband and me.

Two weeks after Reverend Childress asked me to place my hand on my abdomen while he prayed for me, I had a doctor's appointment for my yearly exam and Pap smear. The doctor examined me and said that he wanted to do an ultrasound. He had detected a growth in my uterus. Following the ultrasound, he told me that there was indeed a growth but that he believed we should just watch it for a few weeks and see what happened.

Several weeks later I returned to the doctor for another ultrasound, and he told me that the growth had shrunk. "We will do another ultrasound next year, but it is my belief that it will be gone by then."

"I'm sure it will be," I replied as I gave thanks to God for the healing prayers of Reverend Childress. The following year the growth was gone.

Two weeks after my first visit to the gynecologist, I had an appointment with my ophthalmologist. He examined my eyes and then he asked his assistant to bring him a more powerful lens so that he could better see into my right eye. The assistant brought him the lens, and again he examined my right eye. He did this two other times, each time asking for a stronger lens.

Finally he said, "It appears to me that you have had the beginning of a torn retina, but it looks to me as if it has sealed itself. We will watch it carefully."

Again I gave praise to God for my healing and for Frank's. It seemed that my healing was taking place slowly but steadily, and I could only assume that Frank's was also.

I Think God Intended for You to See This Doctor

During the eight months following my husband's heart attack, our daughter made three appointments for her dad with a doctor at Emory Hospital in Atlanta – a doctor who was ranked in the top ten cardiologists in the United States. Three times she made an appointment, and three times her father canceled. Then one day I came home from work to find that my husband had packed our bags and intended to drive three and a half hours to Atlanta to visit our daughter and grandchildren.

"No," I said, "we are not. You are not able to make the trip."

"I'm going," he said. "If you don't want to go, that's okay." Of course, I went. I couldn't allow him to go alone. When we got to within two blocks of our daughter's house, my husband pulled the car over to the curb, turned to me, and said, "I want you to understand that I won't be going home, but everything you need to know about selling the funeral home is in the bedside table."

My husband could have said, "It looks like rain this evening." His words went right over my head. After making this statement, he drove on to our daughter's house and went in as if nothing was wrong.

Just a few hours later, after climbing the stairs to the guest bedroom, Frank suddenly began having chest pains and announced that we needed to take him to the emergency room. When we got to the hospital, who was on call but the very doctor that he had three appointments with and had canceled all three. "I believe God intended for you to see this doctor," I said. A test showed that my husband was only minutes away from a second major heart attack that he would never have survived.

Three days later, after Frank had heart surgery for several by-passes, we returned home. I thought about the prayers of Ron Childress. I thought about my prayers and the prayers of our son and daughter as we laid hands on Frank the night of his heart attack. We had made God our refuge, and he had been our ever-present help in time of trouble. God had heard our prayers and had worked a miracle. He had given the doctors at Emory the gift of healing.

This story has a beautiful ending. After my husband recovered from open-heart surgery, we sold the funeral home, and he retired. Many people commented that they were sad that he had to sell the business. I always replied that I was sad that he had suffered the heart attack but was not sad that he had decided to retire. After all, he had worked since he was a very young child. At the age of seven, he had left home and gone to live with a widowed school teacher who had a large farm and needed help with all the farm chores. He had bought his first suit of clothes that year. When he was ten, he also began working after school and on weekends in a grocery story bagging groceries. When he was old enough to drive, he drove a school bus after school, and on the weekends and in the summer he worked in Cherokee at restaurants or motels. He never really had a childhood. "Now," I told them, "he will finally have time to play! He will just have bigger toys."

His toys became a truck and a forty-foot RV which allowed

us to travel extensively. Our summers were spent in the New England states and our winters out west. During this time we were able to see every state, Canada, and Mexico. Wherever we were our children and grandchildren joined us allowing us to make wonderful memories and provide many great educational experiences for them.

Frank and Ann in front of their RV
on one of their many trips

Not only had God given Frank back to us, he had given him time to play with his children and grandchildren. Daily I praise God for this wonderful gift.

You Can Do All Things through Christ Who Strengthens You

After I had been in Madison County for two years, the Madison County school superintendent suffered a heart attack. One morning I walked into the central office and was told that I had been named Superintendent. I felt overwhelmed! They had not offered me any more help. I was now to do my job as assistant superintendent *and* that of superintendent. Walking into my office, closing the door, and leaning my back against it, I knew this was the time to claim one of God's most powerful promises.

> "...do not fear, for I am with you, do not be afraid, for
> I am your God; I will strengthen you, I will help you,
> I will uphold you with my victorious right hand."

Isaiah 41:10 NRSV

What a promise! I am your God. I will strengthen you. I will help you. I will uphold you. I couldn't ask for anything more. Hanging up my coat, I got down to business knowing that I could do the job that had been given me.

For the next two years, I did the job of superintendent and continued to fulfill the duties of assistant superintendent. Those were long and sometimes difficult days. My plate had been full before the superintendent got sick. Now my workload had doubled. In spite of this, I don't ever remember feeling exhausted or down. There was always a feeling of exuberance – of elation. I couldn't wait to get to work each morning to see what God was going to do for us that day. It seemed that each day he worked yet another miracle. Every day he was there for me, helping me, strengthening me, upholding me. The verse from Philippians 4:13 NRSV was always on my mind, "I can do all things through him who strengthens me."

One Extra Chair

There was one thing that was a constant for me while working in Madison County. Anytime that I had a meeting in my office, there was always one extra chair. In other words, if there were eight of us meeting, then there would be nine chairs, and that extra chair was placed next to me. That chair was for the Lord! There were times when, during a meeting, someone else would come in and try to sit in the empty chair. I would say, "This chair is taken, but I will get one for you." Because the Lord was always with me I never ever had a serious problem. There were times when individuals entered my office with a great deal of anger and hostility, but when they left, the issues had been resolved, and they were no longer upset. There were times when problems arose for which there seemed to be no solutions, and yet, when we met to discuss them, ideas flowed and solutions were reached. The Lord never failed to help me in every way in every situation.

Several years after I retired as Superintendent of Madison County Schools, I heard of another woman who also made sure that there was always one extra chair in the room. This young woman's husband had left her to rear their three small children alone. When it happened, she was devastated. She didn't know if she could do the job required of her. So she did all she knew to do. She turned to the Lord for help. She told him that if he would always be with her and help her with every decision and in every situation, she knew everything would work out fine. As a constant reminder that he was always with her, she made sure one extra chair was always near, especially at the kitchen table where they ate all their meals and the children worked on their school work.

As the years went by, her children grew to be fine Christians who, like their mother, depended on the Lord. "I could never have made it without the help of the Lord," she says. "Knowing he was always with me made all the difference. I could make decisions knowing that they were right because I trusted him to guide me.

The Grant

My last year in Madison County I heard of a federal grant worth one and a half million dollars. It seemed a godsend to the students of Madison County, but there was only one problem. The grant proposal was due ten days later. I knew what that money could do for the school system, and I knew I had to try for that grant money. I was told that there was no way I could possibly write a federal grant in ten days. I also knew that the person who told me that had no idea what God had done for me in the past and what he could do now or in the future. And so for the next ten days, I did my job in Madison County during the day, and at night I worked on the grant. The result was little or no sleep. My husband and friends worried about me, but I knew that with God's help I could do it and be fine. I knew this because I had done such things many times in my seven years at Blue Ridge. I had been doing this for the past few years in Madison County. On the tenth day, I put the grant in the mail. A few weeks later we received a call that we had gotten the money!

Once I was notified that we had received the 1.5 million dollars in grant money, my busy days only got busier. The proposal I had submitted involved every school in the county;

principals, teachers, parents, local agencies, outside agencies had to be notified, and work had to begin. On top of all this, the school board decided to play devil's advocate. Could part of the 1.5 million not be used for new school construction? Perhaps it could be used for school renovation? My answer to both questions was, "No." During my ten days of writing the grant, I had held meetings with school board members, principals, county officials, and anyone and everyone who needed to have a part in the planning process. I carefully explained the guidelines of the grant and made it clear that the monies could not be used for construction of new buildings or renovation of existing buildings. The money could only be used for such things as after-school tutoring programs and staffing to keep the schools open in the evenings so that parents and students could use the computer labs and libraries. I had shared my vision and asked for their ideas and input. I wanted this to be a community effort that everyone would buy into. When the meetings were over, I felt I had accomplished that goal. But now it was as if the board had heard nothing that had been said. During this time a political cartoon appeared in the newspaper in which I was presiding over a board meeting, and the topic being discussed was the grant. I have to admit that I actually enjoyed the cartoon, and the artist had made me look much better than I actually did!

In the end, after much discussion (on the school board's part) and prayer (on my part), the guidelines of the grant proposal were fulfilled and in the years that followed things went well thanks to Kathy Ray, a very talented young administrator in whose care I left the grant. God had once again gotten me through a difficult time.

Do Not Be Anxious About Anything

"Do not be anxious about anything, but
in everything, by prayer and petition, with
thanksgiving, present your requests to God."

Philippians 4:6 NIV

Eight years after my husband's by-pass surgery Dr. Paul Robinson, the wonderful physician who had cared for him all those years, was diagnosed with leukemia and forced to take a leave of absence. We were heartbroken for Dr. Robinson and his family, and daily we prayed that his health would be restored. I must confess that I also selfishly prayed daily that he would be able to return to work and would be able to continue to see Frank. However, until that day came, we had to find another doctor. I called Dr. Robinson's secretary, and she made an appointment with another cardiologist for Frank's next six-month checkup.

When the day of the appointment arrived, we drove to Atlanta and met with the new doctor. For the next hour, we told him everything that Frank had gone through, the medications that he took, the foods he ate and did not eat, etc. etc. The doctor made no notes and asked few questions. It soon became clear that he had not read Frank's chart before we got there and basically had nothing to say. We had wasted our time in making the trip. After returning home I called Dr. Robinson's secretary and told her everything that had gone on during our visit with the new doctor and asked if she could possibly give us an appointment for the next six-month checkup with a doctor that would be more helpful.

Six months later we again made the three-and-a-half hour drive to Atlanta to meet with another new doctor. From the moment the new physician walked in, we knew that he had studied Frank's medical history. He asked questions, made notes, changed several medications, and insisted that Frank be put through an extensive regiment of tests. We thanked the doctor for his time, told him we would consider his recommendations, and left.

As the six months quickly passed, I became more and more concerned about Frank seeing that same doctor again. The thought of him having to be subjected to so many tests did not really seem necessary. He was doing really well, and there were risks involved with the tests the doctor wanted to order. It was now Friday, and Frank's next appointment in Atlanta was Monday. When I have a lot on my mind, I clean house. The greater my concerns, the harder I clean. I was now vacuuming and praying, doing loads of laundry and praying, and cleaning out closets and praying.

"God, we need your help. We have gone from one extreme to the other with doctors. The first doctor had no recommendations for Frank, and the second doctor wanted to drastically change many of his medications and run an extensive battery of tests. We do not know which doctor is correct. We do not know what to do. Please help us!" I prayed. Suddenly God made it very clear to me that I was to call Dr. Robinson's secretary and ask if there was any possibility that Dr. Robinson was now able to work one day a week. If so, perhaps he would be able to see Frank. I immediately stopped what I was doing, picked up the phone, and called.

"Barbara, I don't suppose that by any chance Dr. Robinson is able to work one or two afternoons a week and could possibly see my husband?" I asked hopefully.

There was a pause and then she said, "Dr. Robinson will see you Monday at one o'clock."

I hung up the phone and went to my knees in thanksgiving! God had again worked a miracle in our lives!

On Monday afternoon at one o'clock, we were sitting in Dr. Robinson's office when he walked in. After hugs all around and inquiries as to his health, we thanked Dr. Robinson for his willingness to see us. "You are quite welcome," he said. "It is good to be back at work and you, Frank Melton, are my very *first* patient upon returning." At that moment I had "goose bumps on my goose bumps," as my mother used to say! It was at that moment I realized the magnitude of this miracle!

After examining Frank, Dr. Robinson said that everything looked good.

"The doctor I saw six months ago suggested that I have a battery of tests done," Frank told him. "Do you feel that any of them are necessary?"

"You do not need any tests. You're doing great!" Dr. Robinson assured him.

"That same doctor also recommended that I go off the blood thinner, but I did not follow his recommendation."

"Good, because you should never go off the blood thinner. For you, I believe that it is critical that you always remain on this medication."

Frank, of course, continued to follow the recommendations of Dr. Robinson and continued to improve. God had watched over us and had not allowed us to make errors in judgment that could have adversely affected Frank's health.

Pray About Everything

As you can tell, I pray about everything. In my opinion, nothing is too small or too insignificant to talk to the Lord about. He is our Heavenly Father, and I believe he likes to hear from us. These are things that I would talk to my earthly father about, and I know that my Heavenly Father loves me even more than my earthly father. Not only that, but I believe God's words when he said, "Do not worry about anything, but in everything by prayer and supplication with thanksgiving let your requests be made known to God." (Philippians 4:6 NRSV)

I will never forget one particular week in February of 1982. On Tuesday, our two teenage children, Myra and Buddy, were out of school because of snow and had gone skiing. About one-thirty I received a phone call from my daughter's friend. "Myra was skiing," he explained, "when another skier hit her and knocked out her two top front teeth."

"Tell Myra to keep the two teeth in her mouth and keep her mouth closed," I said, gathering up my coat and car keys and preparing to brave the icy roads. "I'm on my way to get her."

Now you must understand that Myra had just gotten her braces off the week before. As I drove to the ski lodge, all I could think of were the years she had suffered permanent teeth extractions, braces, and the soreness that accompanies all of this. Now, the very next week after getting the braces off, the top two teeth had been knocked completely out. My heart ached for her. "Okay, God," I prayed, "we are going to need your help. I've called the dentist, and he is going to see Myra the minute I get her to his office. Please give him the wisdom and understanding that he needs in order to know what to do to save her teeth. Please, God, let her teeth be fine."

The dentist put her teeth back in her gums and put something around them to hold them in place. "We'll just have to wait and see what happens next," he explained. "We won't know for a while." We left the office filled with apprehension and hope.

On Thursday of the same week, school was back in session and our son, Buddy, was at wrestling practice. About four o'clock in the afternoon, I received a call from his coach. "Buddy's just gotten his front two bottom teeth knocked out," he told me.

"But he has braces on his teeth!" I exclaimed. "How could his teeth get knocked out if he's wearing braces?"

"Oh, the teeth are still in the braces!" he assured me. "It is the strangest thing I've ever seen. The teeth, the metal bands around the teeth, and the wires are sticking out of his mouth about an inch!"

For the second time in a week, I picked up a child with a tooth injury and headed to the dentist's office. As I drove, I prayed, "We're back again, God, with the same problem. Please let the dentist be able to get the teeth back into place, and please let them remain healthy. Please give the dentist the wisdom and understanding to know how to save those teeth." Once again, we left the office hoping for the best.

That week in Sunday school when the teacher asked for prayer requests I asked the ladies in my class to pray for my children's teeth. That was many years ago and today, both children still have all their beautiful front permanent teeth thanks to the grace of God!

In Philippians 4:6 LB it says, "Don't worry about anything; instead, pray about everything; tell God your needs and don't forget to thank him for his answers." I have committed this verse to memory.

Rosalind Goforth wrote, "There is nothing too great for His power, and nothing too small for His love." This I truly believe. I also encourage you to write down the answers to your prayers as they come so that your faith will grow, and you'll be reminded to thank God for what he does for those for whom you pray.

Of course, I do not spend all my prayer time asking God for help. I try to begin every prayer with praise and thanksgiving. All during the day when I see or hear something beautiful, special, or unique, I immediately thank God for eyes to see, or ears to hear, and a mind to comprehend and appreciate it. Be it a flower, a sunset, an early morning mist over the mountains, or the smile on the face of a child, I take a few precious moments to offer a prayer of praise and thanksgiving.

Throughout the day I whisper little prayers of thanksgiving for God's grace and his mercy. I thank him for the blessings and miracles that he continues to pour out on my family and me. I encourage readers to read a Psalm every day. They are filled with wonderful words of praise and thanksgiving.

For example, in Psalm 103:1-5, 8-13 LB it says, "I bless the holy name of God with all my heart. Yes, I will bless the Lord and not forget the glorious things he does for me. He forgives all my sins. He heals me. He ransoms me from hell. He surrounds me with loving kindness and tender mercies. He fills my life with good things!... He is merciful and tender toward those who don't deserve it; he is slow to get angry and full of kindness and love. He never bears a grudge, nor remains angry forever. He has not punished us as we deserve for all our sins, for his mercy toward those who fear and honor him is as great as the height of the heavens above the earth. He has removed our sins as far away from us as the east is from the west. He is like a father to us, tender and sympathetic to those who reverence him."

Psalm 139:17-18 LB reads, "How precious it is, Lord, to realize that you are thinking about me constantly! I can't even count how many times a day your thoughts turn towards me. And when I waken in the morning, you are still thinking of me!"

Psalm 144:1-2 LB says, "Bless the Lord who is my immovable Rock. He gives me strength and skill in battle. He is always kind and loving to me; he is my fortress, my tower of strength and safety, my deliverer. He stands before me as a shield..."

Peace Is the Presence of God

Sometimes the lives of those we love go seriously wrong, and no matter how hard we try to help them, things only get worse. In the end we just have to give the situation over to the Lord. When we finally do so, we find that we are filled with an amazing peace.

Such was the case with my cousin, Mary Katherine, as she tried desperately to help her husband, Frank "Skeeter" Robinson. He had lost his job in middle management at the age of fifty-five. For months he tried unsuccessfully to find another job. During this time he began to seriously gamble. The deeper he slipped into depression the more he gambled. Mary Katherine got him professional help again and again, but he would never continue with any program.

During this time she began to fear for her life. She would find bullets in the kitchen window above the sink, on her bedside table, everywhere she frequented. She would wake up in the middle of the night to find him standing in the door staring at her. Finally, she obtained a legal separation, moved out of the house, and got a restraining order against him. However, he stalked her day after day. She told law enforcement repeatedly, "It is not *if* he will kill me; it is *when*!"

To support his gambling habit, Skeeter got caught up in some illegal activities which brought him incarceration for months. This was followed by multiple suicide threats, suicide attempts, and a stay in a mental hospital.

One evening, Mary Katherine just gave the entire situation to the Lord. "Lord, I don't know what else I can do to help Skeeter. I fear for my life and for his. I just give all this to you, Lord."

"The moment I prayed that prayer, a warm feeling came over me, and I was filled with great peace."

Weeks went by and Skeeter finally lost everything. His debts became insurmountable. He felt that all hope was gone, and he decided that suicide was truly his only option. One afternoon he crashed through Mary Katherine's back screen door with a gun in each hand and announced that he was going to kill them both. "I love you but I must end my life and I'm taking you with me." He made her walk with him upstairs to the bedroom and stand before the mirror. "You must now decide if you want an open or closed casket because I am going to either shoot you in the chest or the head," he stated as he pointed the gun at her with violently shaking hands.

But God was with her that day. Just at that moment, the phone rang. Skeeter told her to answer it and to get rid of the caller because he wanted no interruptions. It was the guidance counselor at the school where Mary Katherine worked calling to check on her. When her friend heard Mary Katherine speak, she immediately knew something was wrong.

"Is Skeeter there with you?" she asked.

"Yes," Mary Katherine replied.

"Are you in danger?" Deborah wanted to know.

"Yes."

"I don't know your house number to tell law enforcement!" Deborah cried.

In that moment, the peace that God had given Mary Katherine filled her with great assurance. "I had this unearthly feeling of being completely separated from Skeeter even though we were only a couple of feet apart. It was an awe-inspiring sensation. I began to breathe easier and one of my grandmother's favorite Bible verses came to me, 'Be still and know that I am God...' (Psalm 46:10 NRSV). In that moment my focus turned to God rather than the situation. I knew he was with me and for me. I trusted him with the outcome."

Suddenly she began to think in an amazing way! "I immediately saw myself as a child standing in a chair at the kitchen counter back home. In front of me was a cookbook and I was preparing lemonade. I could see the recipe clearly. I began to fabricate a conversation with Deborah about a meeting at my school where a group of teachers were to serve refreshments and needed a recipe for lemonade."

"You need my lemonade recipe? Oh, it's simple," Mary Katherine said. "All you need is one cup of sugar. Just one makes it sweet enough. (Pause) Oh, I've always used just one."

Screaming into the phone, Deborah cried, "One? One? Is that the first house number?"

Mary Katherine's response was calm and deliberate as she lowered her voice in order to get Deborah to do likewise so that she couldn't be heard beyond the telephone receiver. "Yes, that much, then you squeeze the juice of two lemons."

Deborah's reaction sounded like relief as she asked, "One, two are the numbers?"

Mary Katherine acknowledged with, "Yes, then I add six cups of water. You can certainly use less but I've found...."

"One, two, six Asher Lane," Deborah screamed into her cell phone as Mary Katherine continued to talk on about the recipe.

"I boil the sugar in the water and then cool it before adding the juice from the lemons, and I really don't think it's a good idea to serve lemonade with doughnuts."

"Help is on the way!" Deborah cried. "Stay on the line with me! Don't hang up!"

"I really need to run," Mary Katherine replied calmly.

"No! Stay on the line!" Deborah begged.

"I don't think you understand. I really do need to run."

When Mary Katherine had hung up the phone, Deborah had begun calling everyone she could think of and asking them to pray for Mary Katherine and to call all their friends to pray as well. Many prayers were immediately sent up.

When the conversation between Deborah and Mary Katherine had started, Skeeter, thinking it was innocent enough, had sat down on the floor with his back against the wall, stretched his legs out on the carpet, and lit a cigarette while holding fast to the shotgun with the pistol lying on the floor beside him.

When he heard vehicles coming up the driveway, Skeeter got up to look out the window. When he did, Mary Katherine bolted for the stairs and didn't dare look back. Half way down the steep stairway she saw the face of a young officer peering at her through the windows in the door. Her first reaction was absolute relief and just as quickly this feeling was replaced with the realization of the possible danger he was in. At that moment the deputy's eyes looked up toward the top of the staircase. It was then that she heard a thunderous ear-splitting noise and saw a bright flash as a bone-crushing blow slammed her from behind hitting her left arm. She had been shot!

Darkness, silence, and pain followed. And then a second shot rang out! This was followed by an eerie silence, and in that moment she knew that the second part of Skeeter's plan had been carried out. He had shot himself.

"Ma'am, just hold on," someone yelled. "We're going to get you out."

"In the silence that followed," Mary Katherine said, "I remember feeling pity for Skeeter and wondering about his soul."

Finally, after what seemed forever, the front door was kicked open and emergency medical personnel began attending to her as detectives swarmed the house.

"That afternoon I became an amputee." Mary Katherine said. "In the days that followed, I rested and allowed the Lord to rejuvenate my spirit. I learned more in those days than any other time in my life. God gave me the strength to forgive and to let loose of all my bitterness and anger. I learned that peace is not the absence of trouble but rather the presence of God."

Mary Katherine, one month before the accident

Lay Your Burdens at His Feet

There are times in our lives when we are fearful, sad, depressed, or worried about things we can't control, and we allow these feelings to consume us. We pray, but peace does not come. In the end we just have to give our problems to God. When we finally lay our burden at his feet, we find that it has immediately been lifted from us and that we have been given peace.

A wonderful example of this is illustrated in a personal experience told to me by Ann Ledford who has three sons. One of her sons joined the navy after graduation. She had always been a very protective mother, but now there was nothing she could do to protect her son except pray. Daily she prayed, and while that made her feel better, she was still not at peace. "I was making myself sick and worrying my husband terribly," she told me. "Finally, one morning while at home alone, I did what I had thought was impossible. I gave my son over to the Lord. 'Lord', I prayed, 'you know how much I love my son. I also know that you love him more. I turn his health, well-being, and happiness over to you. I trust you to care for him as I cannot.' Immediately I was filled with a peace such as I had never known. From that moment on, I have not worried, for I know God is watching over my son."

Why is it we humans struggle so and worry needlessly, when Matthew 11: 28 NIV tells us, "Come to me, all you who are weary and burdened, and I will give you rest"?

Distributing Bibles in China

*T*urning things over to God does not only apply to serious problems or major decisions. It can apply to everyday occurrences. This was never more clearly brought home to me than in the summer my daughter and I spent a month traveling through China. We decided that we would take Bibles with us as we had heard that it was very difficult for the Chinese people to obtain them. However, we also knew that it was against the law to take them into the country. Therefore, we placed them on top of everything in our luggage so that if our suitcases were opened the Bibles would be the first things the inspectors would see, and they would know that we were not trying to smuggle them into the country.

On our trip our luggage was never checked, and we arrived in China with many Bibles. However, the days began to quickly slip away, and no opportunities ever presented themselves for us to give the Bibles away. Two weeks passed and then three. Finally, only a few days of our stay in China remained. "God," we prayed, "you know we have Bibles to give away, but we have had no opportunity to do so. Therefore, we give this problem over to you. We ask that if it is your will that they be given away, that you will help us do so."

While touring in Canton the next day, we visited a baby food plant which had just opened. The people were very proud of this facility as it would mean so much nutritionally to the children of China. That evening at about 9:30 there was a knock at our door. When we opened it, there stood a young man we had met at the plant. He had borrowed a bicycle and ridden for thirty-five minutes to get to us. He had heard that many Americans were not Christians, and he had come to witness to us. What a wonderful evening of Christian fellowship we spent sharing God's love! During the evening the young man reported that before coming to see us he had stopped to visit with a fifty-six year old man and to witness to him. "He was so very happy when I told him about Jesus and his love. However, I was heartbroken that I could not give the man a Bible so that he could continue to grow in the knowledge of Christ. You see, there is a severe shortage of Bibles in this country," the young man told us.

Here was the opportunity we had been waiting for! We had given the situation to the Lord, and he had acted on our behalf. Truly this evening was worth the wait!

Myra and Ann on the Great Wall of China

God Speaks to Us through His Word

My daughter Myra Hargrove, her husband, and their two little boys, Will age six and Sam age three, were vacationing with another family on one of the Abaco Islands that lies in the northern Bahamas just 60 minutes by air from south Florida. Their plane landed on the main island, and they rented a boat to take them to the private island where they would all be staying together for a week. When the two families arrived on the island, everyone was busy getting things put away. When Myra finished unpacking, she and her two sons walked down to the water and sat together on the sand. The boys busied themselves making a sand castle. Suddenly a rogue wave pulled Sam, the youngest, into the water. Myra had only seconds to react. She yelled for Will, the oldest, to run and get his father while she grabbed all that was visible of Sam, which was his hand.

Instantly mother and son were pulled out to sea and forced to the bottom of the ocean where they were tossed and dragged along the rough sandy ocean floor. "It was like being in a washing machine," Myra recalled, "and each time we were taken down we were scraped along the bottom of the ocean!"

"Just when I would think I couldn't possibly hold my breath another second, we were brought up to the surface, but we were too far out to get to the shore. Then almost immediately, we were pulled under the water again where once more we were tossed and scraped along the ocean bottom. I was praying so hard, 'God, please help me to hold on to this child!' At one point, all I was holding onto was Sam's shirt! At another moment, I was able to get my arm around Sam's waist. When I did, he went limp, and I was afraid he was dead! I was having so much trouble holding my own breath that I just knew he had not been able to hold his any longer."

The second time they were brought to the surface of the water, Myra realized that they were a little closer to the shore and that Sam was miraculously alive! She had time to tell Sam that the next time they were able to surface close enough to shore she was going to throw him toward the beach. He was to crawl as hard and as fast as he could out of the water.

It seemed to Myra that it was forever before that happened. Many more times they were forced to the bottom and scraped and tossed like rag dolls. Finally, they were brought to the surface close enough for Myra to throw Sam toward the shore and to make it there herself. When the two were finally able to crawl up onto the beach, Myra was scraped and bruised, and Sam was wearing nothing at all! He had lost all of his clothing during the underwater struggle.

Myra got the two of them back to the beach house. After she and Sam were bathed and dressed she slipped away from the cabin. "I just had to get away by myself to spend time with God to thank him for saving Sam's life!" she said. She took her Bible with her. As she sat down she thought, "How do I begin to adequately thank him?" She then did something that she often does when she needs an answer. She closed her eyes, opened her Bible, and ran her finger down the page. When her finger stopped, she opened her eyes and read the Bible verse above her finger. It read, "Thanks be to God for his indescribable gift" (2 Corinthians 9:15, NRSV).

God had not only given her the life of her youngest son but had spared her life as well. And, of course, God has given all of us his only Son that we may have eternal life! Truly an indescribable gift!

The following words found in Psalm 116:1-9 LB could easily have come from my daughters lips: "I love the Lord because he hears my prayers and answers them. Because he bends down and listens, I will pray as long as I breathe! Death stared me in the face – I was frightened and sad. Then I cried, 'Lord, save me!' How kind he is! How good he is! So merciful, this God of ours! The Lord protects the simple and the childlike; I was facing death and then he saved me. Now I can relax. For the Lord has done this wonderful miracle for me. He has saved me from death, my eyes from tears, my feet from stumbling. I shall live! Yes, in his presence – here on earth!"

The Bible can speak to you. It is God's word to us and our source of authority for today's world. A close friend told me of a time that she had been deeply concerned about a decision she had to make. She had prayed about it and had not received an answer. Then about three in the morning, she was awakened from a sound sleep and felt led to get up and go to her Bible. Picking it up, she let it fall open at will. The scripture spoke directly to her situation, and she was able to make a decision that left her at peace.

Psalm 119:18-20, 105 LB tells us, "Open my eyes to see wonderful things in your Word. I am but a pilgrim here on earth: how I need a map – and your commands are my chart and guide. I long for your instructions more than I can tell... Your words are a flashlight to light the path ahead of me, and keep me from stumbling."

Myra and Sam a few weeks after their scare in the Abacos

Please Don't Let the Violet Die

*A*s we get older, I believe that our parents consume a large portion of our prayer time. And that is justifiable, as I am certain they spent many hours praying for us, their children. Following is a story I love that concerns a daughter's prayers for her father.

My dear friend Tina Stovall also shares my philosophy of praying about everything. When her father died unexpectedly, she worried that perhaps he had never accepted Christ as his Savior. She desperately wanted to know that he was with the Lord.

Her father had loved African violets. After his death, Tina had kept one of them to remember him by. One day she prayed and asked God to give her a sign that her dad was with him.

Over the next few weeks, the plant bloomed and bloomed. Each day its pot was filled with glorious white blossoms, and Tina gradually realized that it never stopped blooming. "Perhaps this is the sign I have asked God for," she thought hopefully.

Then came the day when she took out a container of what she thought was plant food and dutifully watered all her plants. The next morning when all of the plants looked wilted she realized that she had fed them a mixture of Clorox and cleaner instead of plant food! She immediately grabbed the plants, took them outside, removed them from their pots, and ran clear water over the roots, all the time praying, "God, please don't let the violet die! Please, please, God, don't let this plant die! I don't care about the others, but please don't let this one die."

The amazing thing is that all of the plants died except the violet. Not only did it not die, it never stopped blooming!

Answered Prayer

***M**y* parents divorced when I was two years old, and my mother and I moved in with my grandparents and my aunt in Sylva. When I was seven, my grandfather died, and a few years later my grandmother passed away. My mother moved to Charlotte to attend cosmetology school the year I turned sixteen. It was decided that I would stay with my aunt. My mother later married a man from the Charlotte area and never returned to Sylva. My Aunt Evelyn became the mother figure in my life. We were very close, and I loved her dearly.

Years later my aunt became gravely ill and was admitted to the hospital. When she was stable, I returned to work, but every day I would leave work and spend the afternoon and evening with her. On one particular day, I was met by her doctor the moment I started down the hall toward her room. "Thank goodness you're here. I have been trying to reach you. Your aunt's condition has suddenly become critical. Her vital organs are shutting down. She must be put on life support immediately!"

"Of course," I said.

My husband who had come with me said, "No, Ann, you

do not want to do that. You do not want to put her on life support."

'Yes, I do!" I cried.

At that moment a second doctor walked up and said, "No, you don't." He explained that once a person was put on life support it was almost impossible to have them removed.

Now I was completely confused. I had one person saying that I should put my aunt on life support and two telling me that I should not. On top of that, the first doctor said, "You must decide quickly! You have only about fifteen minutes before it will be too late."

"Do you have a chapel?" I asked.

"Yes, we do. Follow me, and I will show you where," one of the nurses said.

I followed her down the hall where she pointed to some steps that led to a lower level. "The chapel," she told me, "is at the bottom of those stairs."

I walked down the steps and into the chapel where I sank into a pew about halfway down the aisle. "God, please help me," I prayed. "I don't know what I should do. My aunt and I never talked about death and dying. I have no idea what she would want in this situation. Please tell me what I should do. God, please hear my prayer!"

For ten minutes I sat there praying and listening – praying for God's help and listening for his direction. At the end of the ten minutes, I still had no idea what I was supposed to do. At no time had I heard God speaking to me. Never had I felt him leading me in a certain direction. With a very heavy heart, I rose from the pew and began my way up the stairs. When I was halfway up the steps, a nurse appeared and asked, "Are you Ann Melton?"

"Yes, I am."

"You have a phone call," she told me.

I followed her to the telephone. When I answered the voice on the other end said, "Ann, this is Allie Huff. I have had you on my mind all day long, and I just felt that I needed to call you. I don't know if you and your Aunt Evelyn ever talked about death or dying, but she and I talked about it many times. She often told me that she never ever wanted to be put on life support."

I wanted to drop to my knees in praise and thanksgiving to God who had heard my plea and answered my prayer. I had drawn near to God, and he had drawn near to me. I had depended on him to help me, and he had not forsaken me!

I found the doctor and told him what my aunt's best friend had told me. For the next several hours, my husband and I sat with my Aunt Evelyn and talked to her as she slowly passed from this life to her life with God.

On that day God granted me great peace through an earthly voice. For the first time, I truly understood what it meant to be given a peace that passes all understanding. Daily I praise God for that phone call. Daily I think how difficult it would have been to have gone on with my life if I had had to make the decision myself. If God had not spoken to me through my aunt's best friend, I don't believe my life would ever have been the same.

Kay Arthur has a phrase that I love. She says that because we are children of God we are able "to run right into His throne room and find His arms open wide!" Amazing! If we wanted to speak with the president or CEO of some big company, we would have to make an appointment and would probably have to wait a long time. If we wanted to speak directly with the President of the United States, I think our chances of doing so would be slim to none. Yet, we can speak with God any hour of the day or night. What a privilege! What a miracle that on that day, in that hospital chapel, God heard my prayer and caused Allie Huff to call me!

And what a wonderful thing that we don't have to worry about being unworthy or unable to pray as we feel we should. We must just come to God and trust in his grace. I believe that God is always happy to hear from us. Andrew Murray advises, "Pray with the simplicity of a little child. Pray with the holy awe and reverence of one in whom God's Spirit always dwells and prays." In short, just pray!

Since that day, I have become a much better listener. Not only do I listen for God's voice through his word, but I also listen for his voice in the speech of those around me. But more importantly, I believe, I now try to listen more closely for the voice of God directing me to attend to the needs of others. Just as Allie Huff listened to God and followed his urgings, making the phone call that gave me the guidance I needed at a critical time, I pray that I may have many opportunities to do the same and help others in their journey.

Earthly Angel

---

*F*ifteen years after his heart attack, my husband's condition began to deteriorate. On the spur of the moment, I purchased plane tickets to Springfield, Missouri, to take Frank to see our friend Ron Childress, the minister with the gift of healing who had helped us so much after Frank's heart attack.

When purchasing the plane tickets, I was very clear about our need to carry an oxygen generator on board the plane with us. I gave Delta Airlines the make and model of the one we would be bringing with us, and I was assured there would be no problem.

Frank and I drove to Atlanta from Waynesville, North Carolina, and spent the night with Frank's sister who drove us to the airport the next morning. We arrived the usual hour before boarding and after giving the airline our information, we waited. Finally, we heard the call to board and got in line when suddenly a Delta official appeared and told us we would not be allowed to take Frank's oxygen generator on the plane.

"But this machine was cleared when I purchased the tickets," I explained.

"I'm sorry, ma'am, but you will not be allowed to take this on board," the official responded.

"What are we to do? My husband must have this machine!" I cried now with real fear in my voice.

Everyone that was boarding the plane stopped and heads turned in our direction as they listened to this conversation. Each person in line had a look of real concern on his face, and I could hear the comments of many of the passengers. Most were angry and upset with the Delta official.

"You have two choices," the uniformed official replied. "You can stay in Atlanta, or you can go on to Springfield and try to find oxygen there."

"But it's Sunday! How am I supposed to get oxygen or an oxygen generator on a Sunday?" I cried. The man in the uniform only shrugged his shoulders.

"And what is to become of this oxygen generator?" I wanted to know.

"It will go to lost and found," he reported with little or no concern for my plight.

I knew I had to get my husband to Springfield, and so with a silent prayer for help, we boarded the plane. No sooner had we taken our seats when a woman appeared at my side. "I live in Springfield," this woman told me, "and I have a friend there who is on oxygen around the clock. I don't want you to worry. I won't leave you until you have the oxygen your husband needs. As soon as we arrive, I will call my friend and find out the name of her supplier. I know today is Sunday, but perhaps someone will open the business for you. If not, my friend will allow you to use some of her tanks until Monday." With that, she finished by adding, "Now, please don't worry."

True to her word as soon as we were in the airport terminal in Springfield the woman called her friend and got the phone number for the oxygen dealer. We called and another stranger actually agreed to drive several miles into town and rent us a generator. Before leaving the airport, I wrote down the name, address, and phone number of the kind lady who had helped us and put it in a safe place in my wallet. Because of this dear woman, we were able to spend time with Ron Childress and enjoy a wonderful few days.

When we returned from our trip, I opened my wallet to pull out the lady's name and address intending to send her a thank-you note. I emptied my wallet and purse, but the slip of paper on which I had written the information was not there. I could not find her address nor phone number anywhere. It had just vanished!

I even called the oxygen company and asked if perhaps they kept phone records but was told they did not. I was so upset! I decided to call the newspaper in Springfield in hopes they would be willing to put something in the paper that would help me locate this special woman. My call was transferred to a lady who told me that the newspaper actually had a column that perfectly fit my need. "Write your story as concisely as you can and e-mail it to me, and we will run it in our personals column," she told me.

That very afternoon I wrote and mailed the story, which I titled, "In Search of An Angel". I prayed that I would hear something in just a few days. Instead, several weeks went by without any word. Thanksgiving came and went, and then Christmas. Nothing! The day after Christmas we left for Florida for three months, and still I had heard nothing.

Then one day in January, my cell phone rang. "My name is Carolyn Hurt," the distant voice said, "and I am the woman who helped you find the oxygen you needed in Springfield, Missouri. My nephew just called and told me that I needed to look at the newspaper because there was something in there about me!"

she went on. "The reason he knew the article was about me was because you had put in the story that I had been to my aunt's funeral in Knoxville, Tennessee, and was returning home to Springfield."

We must have talked an hour at least! If I had felt blessed when she had helped me in Springfield, I felt doubly blessed now. God had answered both my prayers and had given us not only the oxygen we needed but a wonderful new friend as well!

There are earthly angels among us living their lives in such a way that others can see Jesus in them. Daily they strive to make this life a little easier for others by showing love and compassion for their fellowman. Carolyn Hurt is such a person.

We'll Take It as a Sign and Claim the Promise

Eight years after his heart attack my husband, Frank, walked through the front door of our home and instead of his usual cheery greeting, he went straight to the bedroom and lay down. Concerned, I followed him. "What's wrong?" I asked.

"I'm in terrible pain!" he replied with a grimace, his jaw set and his face ashen.

Picking up the phone, I dialed his doctor while at the same time asking where he hurt and what the pain was like. When the receptionist came on the phone, I told her all I could. She said that I should get him to the emergency room immediately.

Earlier in the day, Frank had had an ultra sound to determine whether or not he had gallstones. The test had shown that he did. Now the emergency room doctor told us that if a patient has gallstones, the ultra sound itself can bring on a gallbladder attack. After studying Frank's earlier test results, the doctor feared that the gall bladder was gangrenous. However, because Frank was on blood thinner, the doctor could not operate for twenty-four hours.

Frank was placed in intensive care, and the anxious wait began. I called many of my prayer partners and activated the deacon prayer chain at our church. Immediately after making that first phone call, I felt the power of prayer begin. God's presence was very real.

At eleven o'clock the next morning, Frank was taken down to surgery, and the surgeon was able to remove the gall bladder laproscopically. With this non-invasive procedure, only three small abdominal incisions were required, and all the work was done through those. However, the doctors uncovered a more serious problem. Frank's bile duct was found to be blocked and was, in fact, worse than the gall bladder had been.

Once Frank was back in ICU, the doctor began giving him large doses of antibiotics and told us that he would have to be taken back to surgery that evening. The surgical team would have to go down Frank's throat and through his stomach to reach the bile duct and try to open it. The doctor did not feel that Frank would have to be put to sleep again for this procedure.

At eight thirty that evening, Frank was taken back to surgery. However, when the doctor was ready to begin the procedure, Frank's breathing and oxygen levels were noted to be unsatisfactory. Because of his heart condition, the doctors felt that it would be safer to put Frank to sleep again even though he had been under anesthesia only seven hours before.

By eleven thirty that evening, the doctors had still not been able to clear the bile duct because of Frank's severe diverticulitis. By the next morning, Frank was extremely jaundiced, and his liver function was at a critical level. The doctors explained that they could not wait any longer. "We must act immediately," they told us. "The bile duct must be opened."

Our doctor told us that he had been working and praying all night to discern a way to get the bile duct open. "I have come up with an idea," he said, "but I don't know if it will work. We can only pray that it will. We will try once again to open the duct. You must understand that if we can't then we have no choice but to do it the old-fashioned way which is major surgery."

"If we have to do that," another doctor said, "it will not be good. Because of his heart condition, it will be risky. Your husband will come out of surgery on a ventilator and recovery will be long and difficult."

By now, I had been in hospitals and around surgeons enough that I could read between the lines. The situation was critical, and Frank was being put to sleep for the third time in twenty-four hours – something that would be hard even on a well person.

Before leaving the room, the doctor held Frank's hand and mine and prayed with us. He also told us that he and his wife had prayed about the upcoming procedure before he had left home that morning. We truly felt that God had led us to this doctor.

At twelve noon on New Year's Day, Frank was taken back to surgery. At one o'clock his younger brother Jimmy, who had been sitting with me in the ICU waiting room, told me that he was going to get something to eat but would hurry back. Just nine years before this, Jimmy had been in the hospital himself for his second open-heart surgery. He had been in surgery for twelve hours. The last three of those the doctor had kept him alive by hand massaging his heart, refusing to give up until the heart started beating on its own.

During those three hours, a spectacular rainbow had come out of the heavens and straight down onto the hospital. It was so unusual and so magnificent that a picture of it appeared on the front page of the local newspaper the next day.

When Jimmy returned from lunch, he walked into the waiting room with the strangest look on his face. "Ann," he asked, "do you remember the rainbow that was over the hospital when I was in such critical condition?"

"Yes," I replied, "I do." That was something none of us would ever forget. "Why do you ask?"

"Well," he said, "there is a rainbow just like that over this hospital right now!"

"Then we are going to take it as a sign and claim the promise!" I exclaimed. At that moment I knew that everything was going to be fine. And sure enough, it wasn't long before the surgeon walked into the waiting room and announced that he had been able to open the bile duct without major surgery. While the doctor was talking with us, Frank was wheeled by looking better than he had looked in days.

We immediately gave praise to God for his mercy. We thanked him for providing us with Christian doctors and for giving the doctors the wisdom and understanding they needed. We thanked him for Christian friends and their prayers. Truly, we agreed, we live under God's rainbow of promises.

Jimmy and Frank with the rainbow behind them

What is Your Rainbow?

Ever since the day that the rainbow appeared over the hospital when my husband was in such critical condition, I have collected rainbow stories. Whenever I meet someone who seems very spiritual to me, I always ask, "What is your rainbow? What gives you hope when things are bad? What provides you the assurance that God is in control?" In the following pages are what I call "rainbow stories." They are the result of my asking many individuals the question, "What is your rainbow?"

A Ladybug

My daughter Myra Hargrove's rainbow is a ladybug. She says that when she sees a ladybug and looks at the tiny dots on its back, she is reminded of how attentive God is to the most minute details. "If God is so attentive that he took the time to put tiny dots on the back of a ladybug," she says, "will he not be even more attentive to and concerned about the details of my life? When problems arise, I have only to think of the ladybug and know that God is at work in my life and will help me through each difficult situation."

A Butterfly

A dear friend Shelva Calloway, who lost her husband to cancer leaving her with four small children to rear, gave me one of my favorite rainbow stories.

"My rainbow," she told me, "is a butterfly. It reminds me that God can make something beautiful out of our lives. No matter how we struggle he promises to be there for us. I once read a story about a man who found a cocoon and placed it on a windowsill to watch. One day he saw that a small opening had appeared in the cocoon so he watched it off and on throughout the day, observing how the butterfly struggled to get out. He decided that he would help the butterfly, so he took a pair of scissors and made the hole in the cocoon larger. When he did, the butterfly emerged easily. The man continued to watch the butterfly because he expected that at any moment the wings would expand. But that did not happen. In fact, the butterfly spent the rest of its life crawling around with a swollen body and shriveled wings. It was never able to fly.

"What the man did not understand was that the restricting cocoon and the struggle required for the butterfly to get through the tiny opening were God's way of forcing fluid from the body of the butterfly into its wings so that it would be ready for flight once it achieved its freedom from the cocoon.

"Sometimes struggles are exactly what we need in our life. If God allowed us to go through life without any obstacles, it would cripple us. We would not be as strong as what we could have been, and we could never fly. So, for me, the butterfly is my rainbow. "

A Flower Garden

"My rainbow is a flower garden," a lady once told me. "When I look at my flower garden, I think how the flowers come from such tiny seeds. Yet with just a little food and water they are able to grow into beautiful creations. And I know that even if a storm comes and destroys my garden or if frost kills it, the perennials will be back again in the spring. I know that this is how it is with God. If we will just give him our heart and a little of our time, he will water us and feed us and turn us into more beautiful creations. No matter what storms we face in life, he will renew us. We only need to have faith in him."

The Dandelion

"Have you ever really studied a dandelion?" a friend once asked me. "You should because you can see God in a dandelion. My husband would probably disagree with me on this. I am sure he sees only a weed. But I see God. In summer, bright bursts of color are everywhere — just as God is everywhere. If you look closely, you will notice that the brightest part of the flower is the center. If you center your life on God, your life will be brighter too. Toward the end of the dandelion's life, the flower becomes even more lovely as it goes to seed, and the wind carries those seeds far and wide. Just as the Good News of Christ has spread, so do these seeds, and the dandelion, like Jesus, lives on.

"Just as Jesus could be found with sinners as well as in his father's house, so the dandelion is found in ditches, weed patches, and on the most manicured lawns. And even with the best weed killer, the dandelion is still around. So just as the world tried to end the life of Jesus, through his resurrection, he is still in the world today.

"I think the dandelion is an amazing flower. The dandelion is my rainbow."

Traffic Lights

"Driving has always been a joy for me," a wonderful friend, Beverly Jackson once told me, "and traffic lights are a reminder of God's presence and power in my life.

"I came to this realization one day during an electrical storm that knocked out all the power in town. Chaos ensued as drivers did foolish and dangerous things. When the power came back on and the traffic lights began to work again, order resumed. It was then that I realized that God gives us traffic lights. The red lights are the 'thou shall nots', the yellow lights are his message to us to be careful and take time to pray things through, and the green lights are his commands to 'go ye therefore and teach all nations.... .'

"I also once saw a wonderful little card," she told me, "that I think perfectly illustrates the message of the traffic light. I don't know who created it, but I am sure he had God in mind when he did. As you will see below, it shows order coming out of chaos."

Chaos
Chaos
Crder
Order

Old Family Photographs

"I collect old family pictures," a gentleman once told me. "I have them all around my house. They are comforting to me. Over the years my home, family, and friends have remained the most important things in my life. I treasure them and I know that I could lose them all tomorrow. Those photographs are a reminder that only God is guaranteed to remain the same. In Hebrews 13:8 LB it says, "Jesus Christ is the same yesterday and today and forever." He is always there for me. I may change. My friends and family may change. My home may change, but God never will. Those old photographs are my rainbow."

Sheep

"My rainbow is a sheep," a woman told me, "and I have one in about every room of my house. You see, I had thyroid cancer several years ago. After I completed all my treatments, my husband and I spent many wonderful days in Ireland where we would awaken each morning to the sound of sheep bleating. It is such a peaceful sound and very comforting. It reminds me that Jesus is the Good Shepherd, and we are his flock. As the Good Shepherd, he will watch over us and protect us. So, my rainbow is a sheep."

A Rock

Collecting rocks is something I do. I pick them up when I hike or travel. I have rocks in every room of my house and placed around the house on the outside. They are a constant reminder to me of God's power, grace, and love. 2 Samuel 22:2 LB says, "Jehovah is my rock, my fortress and my Savior. I will hide in God, who is my rock and my refuge."

My grandmother would always hum as she cooked, cleaned, and worked around the house. The one song I heard her hum most often was "Rock of Ages". Jesus is my rock, and on him I lean. My rainbow is a rock. What is your rainbow?

A Puzzle

One woman's rainbow is a puzzle. "I always have a puzzle spread out on a table in my den," she said. "Each day I work on it. Sometimes, when friends or family come by, they work on it, too. Some days no progress is made on that puzzle. On other days it seems that every piece that is picked up is the right piece and just falls into place. Sometimes I find that, after using all the pieces I have, there is one that is missing. Life is like that, I think."

"My favorite puzzles are those that are three dimensional. But with those you never know exactly what the finished product is going to look like. And with any puzzle you do not know when you begin if all the pieces are even there. You just have to trust that they are. And so it is with life. You have to trust God that our lives are coming together according to his plan. My rainbow is a puzzle."

A Mountain

My grandmother's favorite Bible verse was, "I will lift up mine eyes unto the hills, from whence cometh my help. My help cometh from the Lord, which made heaven and earth" (Psalm 121:1-2 KJV). Because I live in western North Carolina, I have only to look out my window or step outside to see majestic mountains. When I am stressed I hike into these mountains and feel God wrap his arms around me. Sometimes I will drive up the parkway to an overlook where I get out of my car and sit and pray. I feel so fortunate to live in such a beautiful place where I continuously feel God's power and view his awesome creation. So my rainbow is a mountain.

What is your rainbow?

Accept Christ as Your Savior and Begin Your Walk with Him

I'm not sure just when I became aware of the importance of having God in my life. But in my family, death and dying seemed to be a part of our everyday. Someone was always terminally ill and suffering terribly. It seemed that the moment one individual was laid to rest someone else took his place of suffering and dying. The first death that I remember was my uncle, Frank Crawford, who passed away when I was four years old. He was the only father figure that I had ever known. My parents separated when I was two, and my mother and I moved in with my grandparents. Certainly there was my grandfather, whom I loved dearly, but he was my grandfather. Frank Crawford had been like my father. His was the first funeral I ever attended. He was the first person for whom I ever grieved.

It was during his illness when I watched my elders depend on God to get them through the difficult times that I, too, learned the value of faith and the strength one could gather from our heavenly Father. I watched as friends and neighbors came daily to take on some of the ordinary tasks like cooking and cleaning. I watched as they held those that were suffering and heard them pray for one another. Daily I watched my elders turn to the scriptures for help, for strength, and for peace. I may have been only four years old, but as a young child living with much older people, I did a lot of listening, watching and thinking.

As parents, grandparents, aunts, uncles, teachers, coaches, friends and neighbors, we have a wonderful opportunity to teach, by word or deed, the importance of walking with the Lord. Some of my earliest memories are of my grandmother and grandfather reading their Bibles every night before going to bed. They read their Bibles through every year, and they committed to memory verses that could serve as a source of comfort or help to others in time of need. Many times I heard them counsel one of their children or grandchildren with a Bible verse included. In our home, God was very real.

I pray that God is or will become very real to you. If you have not accepted Christ as your Savior, I invite you to do so at this time.

Becoming a Christian only requires that you recognize your need to be saved. Romans 3:23 tells us that we have all sinned and come short of the glory of God. You must also understand that you cannot save yourself. Titus 3:5 KJV says, "Not by works of righteousness which we have done, but according to his mercy he saved us..."

Next, you must recognize that Jesus has provided for your salvation by dying on the cross so that you might have forgiveness from sin and receive eternal life. Christ has paid your sin debt in full. John 3:16 KJV reads, " For God so loved the world that he gave his only begotten son that whosoever believeth in him should not perish but have everlasting life." And finally, you must accept Christ as your Savior. Acts 16:31 NRSV tells us that we must simply believe on the Lord Jesus Christ, and we will be saved. Romans 10:9-10 KJV says, "That if thou shalt confess with thy mouth the Lord Jesus and shalt believe in thine heart that

God hath raised him from the dead, thou shalt be saved. For with the heart man believeth unto righteousness; and with the mouth confession is made unto salvation."

If you wish to accept Christ as your savior just quietly whisper this prayer:

Lord, I know that I have sinned, and so I come to you now asking you to come into my heart so that I may have forgiveness of my sins. I believe in you, Jesus. I believe that you died for my sins. Thank you for your willingness to suffer and die that I might be cleansed and have eternal life. Please help me now as I begin this new journey. Show me the ways that I should go. Help me to grow in faith daily.

Amen

Author's Statement

*T*his book is deeply personal and is taken from my journals. I know that even though I was encouraged by many to write this book, I will get criticism for publishing something so personal. But it is my belief that we are here to praise God and to serve him. I believe that we are all travelers along a difficult road and that as Christians we have a responsibility to help others in their journey. If this book helps even one person, I have achieved my goal.

"Publish his glorious acts throughout the earth. Tell everyone about the amazing things he does. For the Lord is great beyond description, and greatly to be praised" (Psalm 96:3-4 LB).

My Prayer

My prayer for all readers comes from Colossians 1:9-12 NRSV:

I will never stop "praying for you, asking that you be filled with the knowledge of God's will in all spiritual wisdom and understanding, so that you may lead lives worthy of the Lord, fully pleasing to him, as you bear fruit in every good work and as you grow in the knowledge of God."

"May you be made strong with all the strength that comes from his glorious power, and may you be prepared to endure everything with patience, while joyfully giving thanks to the Father, who has enabled you to share in the inheritance of the saints..."

Amen

Bibliography

Chambers, Oswald. *My Utmost for His Highest.* Grand Rapids: Discovery House Publishers, 1992.

Goforth, Rosalind. *Goforth of China.* Grand Rapids: Zondervan Publishing House, 1937.

Graham, Billy. *Angels: God's Secret Agents.* Garden City, New York: Doubleday & Company, Inc., 1975.

Murray, Andrew. *Abide in Christ.* New York: Grosset & Dunlap. 1904

Murray, Andrew. *The Ministry of Intercession in The Andrew Murray Collection.* Uhrichsville, Ohio: Barbour and Company, Inc. 1995.

Murray, Andrew. *With Christ in the School of Prayer in The Andrew Murray Collection.* Uhrichsville, Ohio: Barbour and Company, Inc. 1995.

Myers, Ruth and Warren. *31 Days of Prayer.* Multnomah Books, 1997

Tozer. A. W. *The Pursuit of God.* Harrisburg, Penn.: Christian Publishing, Inc., 1948.

CPSIA information can be obtained at www.ICGtesting.com
Printed in the USA
BVOW031955090713

325466BV00002B/205/P